The Programmer's Guide
to
Quality Assurance

DAVID PALLMANN

FIRST EDITION

DEDICATION

This book is dedicated to the 18+ million software developers in the world, many of whom struggle with quality issues.

ACKNOWLEDGMENTS

This book could not have been written without several decades of software project experience and the learning that came from working on teams as small as 2, and as large as 400. To those who have worked over/alongside/under me on projects since 1979, I thank you for what you have taught me.

I am grateful to Byron Goodman, National Director of Quality Assurance at Neudesic, who provided technical review and made valuable suggestions; and to Becky, Susan, and Debra Pallmann who provided proofreading.

CONTENTS

Contents

Contents

Contents

Contents

Contents

Contents

Contents

INTRODUCTION

This is a book for software developers about quality assurance. Most books on quality assurance, naturally enough, target QA professionals; and for this reason most developers find them dry and uninteresting, or difficult to connect with. This short book, in contrast, is written for programmers by a programmer.

The state of software quality today is, well, pretty awful. Your average software project has far too many bugs—and far too many developers willing to accept that as normal; but there's a ray of hope: you. The mere fact that you've cracked this book open is a good sign: it tells me you're at least *curious* about improving the quality of what you code. Let's take that and run with it: you can be part of the solution instead of part of the problem.

Writing software is hard work, and after investing all that work you certainly want your creation to be successful. This book can help you achieve that by teaching you some things about testing your own work more thoroughly and intentionally improving its quality.

This is not a book about Test Driven Development or any particular software development methodology. You'll find principles within that can help you improve the quality of what you build no matter which software methodology you're using. I will warn you however that if you adopt the guidance in this book, it will change how you develop, how you test, and how you allocate your time. Your teammates will wonder what happened to you, and before long they'll want to know your quality secrets.

And who am I, that you should take advice from me? Only someone who has been writing software for a long time. I eventually got fed up with too many mediocre project outcomes, where everyone works hard but fails to deliver a satisfactory result. I vowed to become an agent of change and a force for good in software quality.

Organization

Part I is about taking ownership of the quality process. As a developer, you are <u>the</u> key ingredient in software quality. While others on your team can influence quality, what you do matters most since you actually produce the software.

Part II is about testing your own work, and testing it well. Failure by developers to sufficiently test their own work is the reason projects have high bug counts: the software entering formal test is frequently incomplete and unfinished.

Part III is about learning from your bugs. Those who fail to learn from their bugs are doomed to repeat them. Only by making changes can you escape from a chronic bug problem.

There's a narrative that runs throughout the course of the book: the story of a young developer on the journey to improve software quality. Each chapter opens with another installment of the story.

Since you're a developer, I know some things about you that are likely true. I can safely assume you enjoy designing things and bringing them to life, and take pride in solving technical problems. There are also plenty of things I don't know about you. I don't know how large or small your team is, how your project roles are named, or what software methodology you use. I don't know if you work on the application front end, back end, or both.

Terminology

Let me explain some of the terminology and symbols we use in this book to represent key roles. These should translate readily to roles on your team.

Symbol	Name	Description
DEV	Developer	You and your fellow software developers.
VIS	Visual Designer	The person who designs the visual appearance of your user interface.
QA	QA	Your quality assurance group, the persons who provide formal testing.
PRD	Product Owner	The persons who provide the vision and requirements. This could be stakeholders, customers, or business analysts.
USR	User	The target users of the software. It's useful to further subdivide users by persona.

Since Agile methods are so popular today, I use some of that terminology. In case you're not familiar with them, below are some terms you'll encounter.

Term	Meaning
Backlog Item	A feature to be implemented in the software. The product manager creates backlog items and prioritizes them.
COA	Conditions of Acceptance (COAs) are conditions that must be satisfied in order for the implementation of a story to be considered complete and correct.
Epic	A master story, which is decomposed into a series of detail stories.
Sprint	A project work cycle.
Story	A description of a requirement.

Web Site

This book's support web site is http://programmerquality.com. Any corrections will be posted there.

PART I: TAKE OWNERSHIP OF QUALITY

"Quality is not an act. It is a habit." - Aristotle

Developers are often buffeted by the software process, floating and flailing in response to requirements and bug reports and deadlines. Part I is about you the developer becoming an active participant in the quality process, with firmly rooted behaviors and personal standards that exceed anything imposed by others.

Chapter 1 discusses the developer's role in software quality.

Chapter 2 is about how to build in quality to your code.

1 YOUR ROLE IN SOFTWARE QUALITY

"Be a yardstick of quality. Some people aren't used to
an environment where excellence is expected."
—Steve Jobs

Narrative

Once there was a bright young programmer named Jon. Jon loved designing and building software, but something was nagging at him. As he worked on larger projects with more complexity, bugs seemed to quickly get out of hand, and neither he nor his teammates were able to regain control. In one project, Jon reflected back on all the nights and weekends he had worked trying to conquer a mountain of bugs. "All these extra hours haven't really changed anything," he sadly concluded. "Getting quality into software must be more fundamental than the number of hours you work."

One day Jon joined a new project whose team really seemed to have its act together. Jon decided he would become a student of programmer quality and learn from his new teammates.

Jon's first visit was to Ruth, the programmer with the lowest bug count of anyone on the team. "What's your secret?" asked Jon. "Why do you have fewer bugs than anyone else?" Ruth smiled thoughtfully, then looked out the window and gestured to a line of trees in rocky ground that had been turned up and displaced by a recent storm. "Do you see those trees over there? Their roots were not deep, so they were easily uprooted." Then she pointed to the other side of the street, where a line of trees stood tall. "But those trees over there held their ground. Their deep roots gave them integrity. That's how I am about the software I write: I'm a quality gate. That means I don't release anything for formal test until I've tested it thoroughly and have fixed all the obvious bugs."

Jon considered for a long moment, then asked, "But aren't you under pressure to deliver software in a certain time period? What happens when the end of sprint comes and you haven't finished testing and debugging?" Again Ruth smiled. "Do you want to be steamrollered by the quality process or do you want to be an active participant in it?" "An active participant!" said Jon without hesitation. "Well then," continued Ruth, "that requires integrity. Like the trees, there are going to be storms: pressure to deliver the software before it's ready. But if you're a quality gate, your job is to hold firm—that's what gives the quality process integrity.

"I'll admit it was a little scary holding firm at first, but my manager and team have come to realize that getting software sooner rather than later is of no use if it's buggy," Ruth added. "And don't get the idea that I'm constantly late on sprint work. I've improved my estimating. I set realistic expectations for what I can accomplish in a sprint that includes plenty of time for testing and iteration."

"I can see the value of what you're saying," said Jon, "but isn't quality QA's job? With all that extra testing it seems like you're doing QA's job as well as your own." Ruth laughed. "Our QA team is great, but quality is my responsibility—and no one else's! Since I create the software, I'm the only one who can affect its quality."

Who is Responsible for Quality?

Whether you are part of a large or a small software team, there are many hats being worn. Someone is giving requirements, someone is designing a user experience, someone is making platform and architecture decisions, someone is writing code, and someone is testing.

Just who is responsible for quality?

One popular answer that is easy to get behind is "quality is everyone's job", and there's certainly some truth to that: every member of a team, regardless of their role, can *influence* quality. But who, really, is *responsible* for quality? Who on the team is able to *affect* the quality of what is being produced?

Look no further than the nearest mirror. The answer is you, the programmer. Like it or not, you are the deciding factor in the quality of the software. If you build flawed software, no amount of effort or hand-wringing by other roles on the team can fix it. The ship floats or sinks based on what you build.

You might disagree. Perhaps you think quality is the responsibility of your Quality Assurance group; after all, quality is in their name! QA personnel can be tremendously helpful in illuminating where there are issues and what the conditions for failure are—but your QA personnel can only *assess* quality: they cannot *provide* quality.

What about those writing the requirements? Surely the correctness, clarity, and timeliness of requirements affects the quality of the software. Well, it's certainly true that you can't build good software without a proper understanding of the requirements—but it's the developer who is in a position to [politely] point out when requirements are inadequate and [gently] insist they be corrected before work can get underway. You see, it always comes back to you.

So then, quality is everyone's job... but it's mostly your job. Once you have come to accept that, you can put a quality perspective on everything you do. When you are given requirements, confirm they meet your quality bar. When you create a technical design, ensure it's reliable, scalable, and secure. When you write code, make it clean and clear; and accompany it with comments, error handling, and unit tests. Test your work, and test it thoroughly.

Software quality (or lack thereof) is a direct result of how well the developers do their job.

A Tale of Two Developers

What kind of developer are you, and what is your quality reputation? If we tracked programmers like baseball players, what would we see on your "programmer baseball card"? Let's compare two developers side-by-side that way.

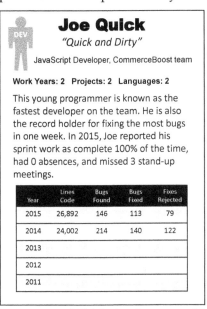

Joe Quick
"Quick and Dirty"

JavaScript Developer, CommerceBoost team

Work Years: 2 Projects: 2 Languages: 2

This young programmer is known as the fastest developer on the team. He is also the record holder for fixing the most bugs in one week. In 2015, Joe reported his sprint work as complete 100% of the time, had 0 absences, and missed 3 stand-up meetings.

Year	Lines Code	Bugs Found	Bugs Fixed	Fixes Rejected
2015	26,892	146	113	79
2014	24,002	214	140	122
2013				
2012				
2011				

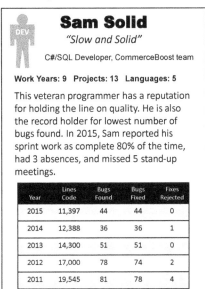

Sam Solid
"Slow and Solid"

C#/SQL Developer, CommerceBoost team

Work Years: 9 Projects: 13 Languages: 5

This veteran programmer has a reputation for holding the line on quality. He is also the record holder for lowest number of bugs found. In 2015, Sam reported his sprint work as complete 80% of the time, had 3 absences, and missed 5 stand-up meetings.

Year	Lines Code	Bugs Found	Bugs Fixed	Fixes Rejected
2015	11,397	44	44	0
2014	12,388	36	36	1
2013	14,300	51	51	0
2012	17,000	78	74	2
2011	19,545	81	78	4

Which developer would you want on your team?

Joe is a young developer who is valued because JavaScript is his first programming language—unlike some of the older members of the team. Joe is very popular with management because he has a reputation for being fast: he is never late with his sprint assignments, and he's written more lines of code than anyone on the team. However, are these the right things to be valuing? It's revealing to take a deeper look at Joe's stats. He has a very high count of bugs found by QA. Although he fixes bugs rapidly, the number of bug fixes rejected is very high. This tells us that Joe is "fast" because he is not really finishing his work completely. His bug fixes are often incomplete and are likely introducing additional bugs as well. Clearly, Joe has some good points but has a lot to learn about quality: his net quality contribution to the team appears to be negative.

In contrast, we have Sam who at first glance does not seem to do as well as Joe in some areas. He's written far less code, he's missed more meetings, and he often doesn't finish his sprint tasks on time. Sam does need to improve his estimating and his attendance, but we can see from his other stats that these delays come from Sam's commitment to finishing his work and testing it well. He has far fewer bugs than Joe, fixes nearly all of them, and his bug fix rejection rate is practically zero. Moreover, Sam's statistics improve each year. This is why he has a reputation for quality. In light of this, we can see the reason Sam writes fewer lines of code: it does not indicate low productivity; rather, he takes the time to get his code clean, right, and nicely factored.

Determine the quality reputation you want to have
and let that drive your behavior.

Be a Quality Gate

In order to make a difference in software quality, you the developer must become an active participant in the quality process instead of merely reacting to it. You need to become a quality gate, meaning you don't take on work you can't deliver on, and you don't release code for testing until it is ready.

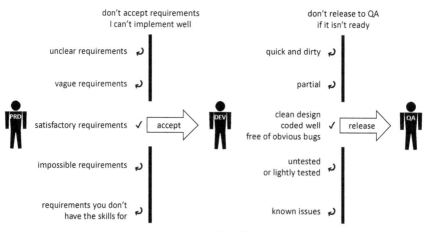

Be a Quality Gate

If a set of requirements is so poorly written, incomplete, vague, or full of contradictions that you can't possibly develop reliable software for it, you must <u>decline</u> the requirement as insufficient. You can do this politely, gently, and constructively; simply point out what the problems are and ask for necessary improvements. Be open to iteration, and be open to partial stories that will be extended later, but do not agree to start work on something that cannot ever work properly. Similarly, you should also reject requirements that require skills you do not have, unless you and your management discuss it openly and decide this is a good opportunity for on-the-job learning of a new skill.

If your code is not known to be solid, you must <u>withhold</u> it from entering formal test. If your design is not clean, refine it. If your implementation is not complete, finish it. If your code is poorly structured, refactor it. If you haven't sufficiently tested the code, test it. If you haven't corrected all obvious bugs, fix them. Only then should you be releasing software for formal test.

Be a quality gate. Do not accept flawed requirements that are so faulty they cannot be implemented, or that you lack the skills to implement. Do not release code for testing that has a questionable design, a weak implementation, or isn't free of obvious bugs.

It's your enforcement of this that is critical. If you aren't already in the habit of pushing back when you need to, it's time to learn this important skill. If it seems unpleasant, think how more unpleasant it is to have poor quality software out there and a damaged reputation—because that's the alternative to a developer not holding the line on quality.

Please note, you can push back without being pushy! Be firm and candid, but not ugly or abrasive. Avoid seeming arrogant or uncooperative. Point out the very real consequences of not having a quality bar vs. the benefits of enforcing one. Express your concerns in a constructive, non-personal way, making it clear you are only interested in the success of the project. Be open-minded and listen to others in your discussions, and others will respond in kind. If you build a reputation as the developer with the greatest passion for quality and the most stable code, you'll be astonished at the level of trust your team will put in you.

Right about now you may be wondering if doing all this diligent testing will slow you down to an unacceptable level; is the quality programmer destined to miss every deadline? Well, it's certainly true that doing a job completely will take longer than doing a job minimally—so yes, there is going to be time impact. On the other hand, consider this: if your bug count is significantly lower than other developers, you're not slower in the long term. In addition, as you develop better quality habits your improved code will require less debug time.

Interactions with Your Team

Now that we've established that you the developer bear the primary responsibility for quality, we can discuss the behaviors of other roles on your team. Their effect on quality is secondary to your own, but your team can have a smoother and more efficient rhythm when everyone is working in concert.

Effective Communication

An effective team depends on effective communication between team members. As a developer, the best way to present yourself is as a professional who is courteous and constructive.

Software projects can result in great pressure and tension between roles at times. You'll be most effective if you strive to be constructive in all of your interactions. Even when you need to be forceful or are in conflict with someone else on your team, you'll win a lot of respect if it's clear to all that you always have the success of the project in mind.

Be constructive in all of your interactions.

Electronic mechanisms like bug tracking systems and requirements repositories can be great aids for a project team, but they are not a replacement for direct person-to-person communication. Augment those electronic systems with real communication. The difference between a functional team and dysfunctional team often comes down to how well team members communicate. A team is not just a collection of talented people; it's a collection of talented people who are able to work together. Think of a team not as an organization but as an organism.

If you are having trouble engaging well with an entire group on your team, try to find one person in the group who you communicate with best and leverage them as a liaison. For example, if you're not connecting well with testers as a group, perhaps one of them has more of a programming background than others, or some other common interest. You'll only learn such things if you take the time to get to know the people you work with.

Communicate regularly with your team members.

Requirements

A big part of assessing the quality of your work is how well it meets the requirements, so it's essential to have good requirements and to understand them.

Adequate Requirements

Capturing and communicating requirements well is neither easy nor commonplace. Requirements originate with stakeholders, and may be further filtered by other people such as business analysts, product planners, or designers. By the time they come to you, requirements have hopefully been expressed in a clear, logical description that is accompanied by conditions of acceptance and a visual design. This won't always be the case, of course: requirements can be too short or too long; may be unclear or ambiguously worded; or even be just plain incorrect at times.

A story should be as long or as short as it needs to be in order to describe the requirement. While overly-detailed stories probably won't get read by everyone, overly short stories that omit important details are no better.

If you don't feel you have been given satisfactory or complete requirements, you can and should stop the train from moving until that is corrected. It wouldn't be reasonable to expect a construction worker to build a house without a blueprint or building codes, nor is it reasonable to expect a programmer to write software without adequate requirements. You should be polite but firm about this. If you are pressured into proceeding anyway, then document the assumptions you are forced to make.

Don't commit to development work if you don't have satisfactory requirements.

Common Understanding

It's extremely important for everyone on a team (not just you the developer) to reach a common understanding of a requirement as early as possible. Nothing is more frustrating than for everyone on a team to work hard only to find out late in the game that each had a different understanding: it means you're not all pulling in the same direction. If the developers don't understand the requirement correctly, they will build the wrong solution. If QA doesn't understand the requirement correctly, they will file bugs that aren't really bugs.

Without a Common Understanding, Mass Confusion Ensues

If your team doesn't have the practice of reviewing and discussing stories regularly, suggest they start doing so. Touch base with the author of your requirements often, and show them your work as it progresses. If your team is distributed geographically, you may also want to consider a wiki or other online mechanism for discussing story details.

Ensure you and your team members have a common understanding of a requirement.

Changing Requirements

This is the age of agile software development, which principally came about in recognition that requirements are always subject to change. That means your requirements are going to change over time (count on it).

In older times when waterfall was the dominant software methodology, requirements were often captured in a single monolithic specification document. When that document changed, its version number was updated. These days, you're more likely to get a collection of *stories* in an electronic repository. Stories have a good side and a dark side. The good side is that stories can be easily updated individually, which allows the requirements to become something of a living document: as understanding improves or changes are needed, requirements can be added, updated, or removed. The good side is also the dark side, because changing requirements can be extremely difficult for developers to keep up with.

Clear and Complete Requirements

The story collection approach can be very sloppy if it is not well-maintained, which raises the possibility of contradictions and duplications. A good story curator will organize groups of stories into epics. As you survey the stories that collectively make up your requirements, be on the lookout for the following problems and bring them to the attention of the story writers:

- Contradictions between requirements. Like a detective, be on the lookout for requirements that seem to make sense individually but are problematic when combined. Are there discrepancies? Are there holes in the story?
- Unspoken requirements that are implied (or mentioned verbally) but not clearly spelled out in a story.
- Complex stories that need to be refined and broken into smaller, simpler stories.
- UI discrepancies between story text, wireframe diagrams, and visual designs.

To minimize misunderstandings, ensure that your requirements are maintained in such a way that there is never more than one edition of the same story out there. There should always be one and only one version of the truth.

Insist on having one version of the truth for a requirement.

When that truth changes, be sure there is a mechanism for developers to be notified. In particular, when you are in a development cycle you want to be aware of story changes during the cycle. Check your requirements carefully when you start work but also regularly re-read them.

If you ever find yourself in the unfortunate position where requirements change drastically or contradict and there is denial about this (or a lot of finger-pointing), you may find it helpful to keep a decision record that documents the requirements and instructions you were given at different times by different people.

Trustworthy Estimates

Trustworthy communication is one of the most valuable gifts you can give your management. When you report the status of a development task or provide an estimate of work, how reliable is it? The status you report influences decisions about deadlines and what to include in a release. If what you communicate is frequently unreliable, that injects uncertainty and undermines planning.

Remember that an estimate is just that: an estimate. It's not intended to be exactly accurate, but neither is it supposed to be off by orders of magnitude.

An estimate quickly goes south when any of the following are true:

- *Unfamiliarity.* You don't understand what you're being asked to estimate very well; or will be using tools or technologies you are unfamiliar with. Be honest about what you don't know.
- *Missing Tasks.* You haven't identified all of the necessary tasks. The unaccounted for tasks are "dark matter" in the estimate. Brainstorming with others about your tasks will help identify what's missing.
- *Insufficient Task Decomposition.* The tasks you've identified are not granular enough. Small familiar tasks can be estimated with certainty; ambitious, complex, or unfamiliar tasks cannot.

- *Dependency Optimism.* Some of your tasks are dependent on completion of tasks by other team members; this creates a kind of "race condition" where your estimate can be derailed if others do not deliver what you need in time. Be up front about dependencies in your estimate.
- *Shallow Task Estimation.* You fail to take into account the *definition of done* for your project tasks. If you only estimate the coding time for a task when you are also expected to write unit tests and test your work, you will underestimate the task. Think through all aspects of a task when you estimate it.
- *Peer Pressure.* You estimate based on the expectations of others ("this shouldn't take you more than a week") rather than what you really think. This is especially common with fixed-time sprints and a product owner's wish to get a certain amount of work achieved in that time. Always give your honest opinion of what you believe you can achieve, not what others want to hear.

Even when you avoid the above pitfalls, estimation is a black art at times. The only way to get good at it is to analyze your estimation performance: when you finish a sprint, revisit your estimate and see how well you did so you can improve your technique the next time around. When conditions change (such as a late-breaking requirement), be sure to update your estimate.

Fully counting the cost is a critical aspect of estimation. No one will mind if you complete your work early; being late causes disruption.

Pursue accuracy in your estimates and become a reliable communicator.

Interacting with QA Personnel

Your Quality Assurance group has the unenviable job of assessing the quality of what the development team produces. While the relationship may be adversarial in some respects, you're all working toward the same goal: delivering a quality solution.

Like stories, the quality of bug reports can vary quite a bit. A good bug report will allow a developer to quickly understand what the issue is, and will also contain sufficient detail to reproduce the problem so it can be worked on. A poor bug report wastes time and impedes productivity.

Format of Bug Reports

Most bug tracking systems have some standard fields (such as title, priority, assigned to) and a text area for the bug description itself. If you can get your team to agree on using a template for bug descriptions, that will help ensure bug reports contain all of the essential elements. Ideally, a bug report will contain many or all of the following (any items that don't apply can be omitted).

- *Title*: a meaningful title, summing up the problem in a short sentence.
- *Area*: Which feature area of the software was being exercised.
- *Assigned to*: person assigned to investigate and resolve the problem.
- *Priority*: a priority for the issue, based on criteria the team has agreed upon.
- *Bug Category*: The type of bug (e.g. Browser, Data/Storage, Functional, Visual, Interaction, Input/Validation, Mobile, Security, and so on). A category field aids in analyzing your bugs to identify where the problem areas are.
- *Description*: a brief summary description that conveys the essence of the problem in a few sentences. Long detail, if needed, can be added to the end of the bug report or attached.
- *Observed behavior*: what the tester observed happen.

- *Expected behavior*: what the tested expected to happen (if possible, indicate which story describes the expected behavior).
- *Repro steps*: the steps that were taken to arrive at the problem. Include details which may be pertinent, such as which environment was being accessed; which version of the software was deployed; who you logged in as; and which browser or device was being used. If the problem only occurs intermittently, be sure to indicate that.
- *Screen captures*: a picture is worth a thousand words. Attach screenshot(s) where possible to show what the tester was seeing.
- *Special conditions for failure*: list any special conditions required to see the problem (for example, specific data entry values).

If you are unable to reproduce a bug report, connect with the tester who filed the issue and ask them to show it to you. Make the bug report more complete based on what you learn.

Here's an example bug report that uses the template described above.

Salary is displaying to 8 decimal digits for US users.
Area: Payroll—Add/Edit Salary Record
Assigned to: Sam Solid
Priority: 1
Bug Category: Consistency
Description: In Add/Edit Salary Record, the Salary field amount is shown to 8 decimal digits for US users.
Observed behavior: Salary amount has 8 decimal digits.
Expected behavior: Salary amount has 2 decimal digits.
Repro steps:
1. Sign in as a user with permissions to use the Payroll module.
2. Navigate to salary records.
3. Edit a record for any employee.
4. Notice the displayed salary amount shows to 8 places after the decimal point.
Screen captures: <attachment1.jpg>
Special conditions for failure: None

Use a standard format for bug reports, so they can be
easily understood and acted upon.

Investigations

Simply documenting that something failed in a bug report is not sufficient: the person filing the bug should also be performing a preliminary investigation.

Which of the following two bug reports would be more useful to a developer?

> Bug Report A
> Import Wizard fails in validation step at 20%
> Description: While running the Import Wizard, after an input file is uploaded, the wizard stops at 20% and does not continue.
>
> Bug Report B
> Import Wizard fails in validation step at 20%
> Description: While running the Import Wizard, after some input files are uploaded, the wizard stops at 20% and does not continue.
> Investigation shows that the problem occurs when certain types of data are imported (see attachments 1 and 2 which fail, and attachments 3 and 4 which do not fail).
> *Bug Report vs. Bug Report with Investigation*

Clearly the second bug report is to be preferred: much more information has been discovered about when the problem occurs, and examples of failing and non-failing input data have been attached for the developer.

When investigating a bug report, considerations like these should be looked at:
- Does the problem occur every time, only under certain conditions, or is it intermittent?
- Is the problem related to a particular pattern of use?
- Is the problem related to a particular browser or device?

- Do user identity and permissions affect the problem?

A bug report should be accompanied by an investigation.

Bug Churn

Ideally, after a tester files a bug a developer resolves the issue and the bug can be verified and closed. Sometimes the interaction goes less smoothly however.

If the developer can't reproduce the bug, it may be reassigned to the tester as "cannot reproduce". The tester can provide additional clarification, or show the problem to the developer, so that the issue can be reproduced and resolved.

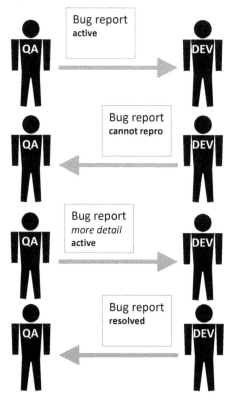

Cannot Reproduce Bug Routing

If QA doesn't agree a bug is fully resolved, the bug may be re-activated and assigned back to the developer. After discussing why QA disagrees, the developer can do a more complete job of resolving the issue.

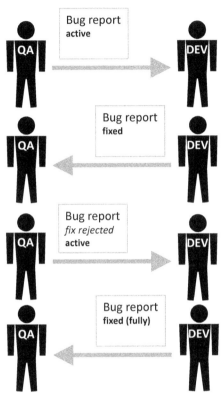

Fix Rejected Bug Routing

This back-and-forth may just be a need for clarification or discussion, but if you find it happening repeatedly it indicates a problem. Perhaps not everyone understands the requirements the same way, or perhaps the way bugs are being reported is not very complete. Perhaps the code fixes are problematic, incomplete, or introduce unwanted side effects. When you see a pattern of bug churn, it's vital to find out why it is happening and <u>put an end to it</u>. If you don't arrest the churn, your team will have the appearance of being busy but will not be making any actual progress.

Recognize dev-QA churn and address it: never mistake motion for progress.

High Bug Counts

Once the open bug count starts to climb, project management can get concerned, resulting in a lot of unpleasant pressure on the development team.

When you find yourself in this situation, the first question you ought to ask is <u>why</u> are there so many bugs?

If many bugs are being logged because stories are not understood the same way across the team, request a team meeting as soon as possible to review and clarify stories.

If the bugs being logged are valid, then you and your fellow developers may not be doing a sufficient job in self-testing. Scan the bug list and ask yourself how many of the bugs you see are obvious ones that the developer should have caught before turning the software over to QA for testing. If the majority of the bugs are in this category, developers are not spending enough time self-testing their work and should allocate their time differently: take on less new work per sprint and spend more time testing and debugging.

If you're seeing a lot of breaking changes or a regression in functionality, you have an insufficient number of automated tests. Automated tests are the best way to safeguard what already works and keep it that way.

Getting your team to agree to a few sound practices in how bugs are logged can also affect the bug count and how it is perceived.

- Before a bug is logged at all, check whether the issue has already been logged.
- Track and prioritize *suggestions* differently from actual defects.
- Set priorities meaningfully and work in priority order, so the most important issues are being addressed first.

- If you see the same issue logged multiple times because it shows up in more than one area of the software, consider consolidating them into a single bug.
- If you encounter a long bug report that is actually describing multiple issues, get that separated into one bug per issue. It's easy to address atomic issues, whereas bug reports that encompass multiple issues (or are vague) can be near-impossible to resolve.

Track bugs efficiently in order to have issues that are actionable and an accurate status.

2 BUILDING IN QUALITY

"Trying to improve software quality by increasing the amount of testing is like trying to lose weight by weighing yourself more often. What you eat before you step onto the scale determines how much you will weigh, and the software-development techniques you use determine how many errors testing will find."—Steve McConnell, Code Complete"

Narrative

Jon's next visit was to Craig, a middle-aged developer who seemed to have everyone's respect for solid code. On his desk was a biography of Michelangelo. "I've been looking at some of the code you've written in source control, and I must say, it's absolutely pristine." admitted Jon. "Your code is so clean it screams quality. Can you tell me why your code looks so much better than anyone else's?"

Craig blushed but eagerly drew up a chair. "A few years ago, I had to extend some code that was several years old. It wasn't written very well: it was overly complex, hard to follow, and had few comments. I couldn't understand how much of it worked, which made it a real nightmare for me. Many of my changes backfired. The worst thing was, I was the author of this code! Enough time had gone by that I couldn't make heads or tails of it." Jon's eyes widened in appreciation. Craig continued, "I decided then and there that I would only write quality code from that point on. Code has to be understandable and maintainable, or it's not worth writing.

"When I write code now, the design must be solid, if not elegant. The code must be cleanly structured without complexity. Oh, it doesn't always start out like that; there are plenty of missteps and rework along the way. But that's how I end up. It takes dedication to good software engineering principles—like Separation of Concerns, DRY, and Defensive Programming; and sometimes a lot of refactoring. The code also needs to be proven by passing tests. Only then am I finished."

"Hmm..." mused Jon. "I have to tell you, I think I am already doing most of those things. Why doesn't my code look like yours? I try to avoid complexity, I refactor..." "You're doing those things, but are you doing them enough?" asked Craig. "What do you mean?" asked a puzzled Jon.

"What I'm asking," said Craig, "is how fully are you applying those software engineering principles? For example, let's take Don't Repeat Yourself. When our team first started discussing DRY a few years back, most of our developers said they were already following this principle and had a good set of classes in place. What we found, though, was that we had barely scratched the surface. We found a code clone analysis tool for our development environment. When we ran it, we discovered we had over 100,000 lines of duplicate code in our project! When we started

thinking about all the ways we could apply DRY, new opportunities opened up all over the place. Our front-end developers replaced our CSS files with LESS files, which allowed us to centralize things like colors in variables rather than repeating them throughout many style rules. Our database programmer started using views to avoid duplicate select statements and joins in stored procedures.

"I'm also asking whether you are finishing the job," Craig continued. "I doubt my first draft of code looks much better than yours, but I refine it and iterate until I am satisfied with it. I guess that's the craftsman in me. I like to picture myself as the sculptor removing all the unnecessary bits from a slab of marble to reveal the masterpiece within. Did you know Michelangelo spent three years on the statue of David and four years on the Sistine Chapel?" Jon admitted he didn't. "It's when your code begins working that you may be tempted to say you're finished—but you mustn't stop before your code is clean and complete and proven."

"Allow me to recap," Jon offered. "You need to use good software engineering principles and apply them fully, but you also need to be a craftsman. You can do all the right things, but if you don't iterate to the finish line you're really only half-done." "Now you've got it!" replied Craig with satisfaction.

Rise Above the Norm: Be a Craftsman

Every day, millions of lines of code are written and much of it is flawed, imperfect, and incomplete. This situation is common but not admirable. Make a pledge to yourself to do better than that: rise above the norm and refuse to produce mediocre software. Set a personal quality bar for your code and enforce it.

How can you make that goal a reality, when no one writes perfect software? When you're up against a deadline? When your requirements are changing all the time? When a lot of code is already written, but defective? While there's no magic wand that will improve the quality of your code overnight, there are changes you can make—starting today—that will make a lasting difference. Commit to becoming a craftsman and improving your code quality; then work at it every day.

> *Be a craftsman. Have a personal quality bar and*
> *don't compromise it.*

Know Your Enemy

It's common in quality assurance circles to portray bugs as the enemy, and discuss techniques to attack these "pests". While there's some value in this, we developers know better. A bug is not some external critter that wriggles its way into your code, it's flaw in our code that never should have been there in the first place. Bugs aren't the real enemy, they're just a symptom of the real problem: ourselves. The root cause of bugs is how imperfect our code is.

We are the problem. Bugs are only a symptom.

If you're in denial about this, if you're one of those programmers with a massive ego, this is going to be humbling to face. But face it you must, if you want quality to improve. The only way you will have fewer bugs is if you make improvements to yourself.

> *Quality problems are developer problems. Bugs are*
> *just the symptom.*

The True Cost of Bugs

Quality matters. Software quality problems can compromise privacy, break laws, mischarge customers, waste millions of dollars, damage reputations, end careers, put companies out of business, and even kill people. Bugs have caused the loss of aircraft, ships and spacecraft; affected election results; flooded the stock market with unwanted trades; disrupted phone service; shut down nuclear reactors; released convicts early; compromised military operations; and almost started wars.

Even when the consequences of bugs don't make the headlines, they often result in a significant loss for someone (indeed, as I write this I am hearing frantic cries of exasperation from the next room; my wife has just lost hours of financial data entry due to a bug in home budgeting software). Losing your day's work or being unable to get a correct report may seem trivial in comparison to the consequences we just mentioned, but they happen on a large scale and a great many people are affected.

The Exponential Cost of Fixing Bugs

Bugs are expensive to fix, and it only gets worse over time: the cost of correcting bugs increases exponentially with each successive stage of the development cycle. The chart below shows some commonly cited multipliers, based on Barry Boehm's 2007 Equity Keynote Address. These findings suggest the cost of fixing a bug discovered in Production can be 150 times what it would have cost to deal with early on.

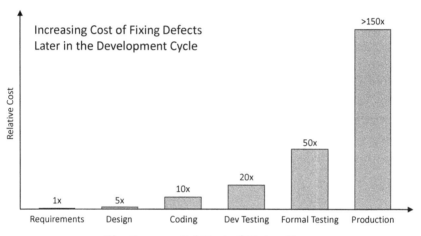

The Exponential Cost of Fixing Bugs

Clearly, the earlier bugs are dealt with the better. Better still is avoiding them in the first place. This means we have to throw away the idea that quality is only something we focus on during a formal test stage. Quality needs to be an up-front, ongoing, continuous, ever-present consideration.

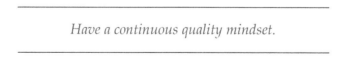

Have a continuous quality mindset.

Imagine if you felt a tiny pin-prick of pain every time a user experienced a bug in software you wrote; how much pain would you be in right now? Our attitude about bugs needs to change. Defects cause a great deal of harm, and it's made all the worse when we fail to learn from our mistakes and end up repeating the same problem all over again. You'll be a far more careful developer if you keep in mind just how severe the consequences of software problems are. We developers need to adopt serious bug prevention and containment measures. A bug that slips past you into formal test should be rare, not a commonplace occurrence.

Treat bugs like the wild animals they are and don't let them escape into the wild, where their effects can magnify.

More Quality in How You Work

Developer testing is important, but testing by itself does nothing to improve the quality of your software; it merely reveals how close (or far) you are from your objective. Quality is the result of your design choices and the correctness of your implementation.

Generally speaking, developers aren't careful enough in their design and construction. A design that is adequate is not the same as a tightened up, optimal design. Draft code is not the same as polished, bullet-proof code. Code that works is not necessarily easily-understood, maintainable code.

Below are some design and construction practices that will help you install a higher level of quality. You are likely familiar with many of these—but are you using them, and using them effectively?

Know Your Limitations

It's when your design and implementation come up short that all those awful bugs ensue. And let's be realistic about this: you *will* get them wrong. Since we're all flawed human beings, your first draft will almost certainly be less than perfect. It will be wrong because you didn't read the requirements carefully; or because your design failed to consider a use case; or because your logic was only partially thought through; or because you got distracted and forgot to write some of the code; or because you weren't careful enough cutting and pasting; or because of a typo you didn't know you made; or because you're using a language or framework or component you don't understand very well; or because you took a shortcut; or because you're having a bad day.

This isn't meant to make you feel bad, only to remind you of how important it is to compensate for our limitations by being disciplined and following good software engineering principles. Avoid overly-ambitious code. You need a solid design, good code structure, and sufficient testing. It's difficult to be successful without them.

Recognize your limitations and avoid being overly ambitious.

Test, Refine and Iterate

The bad news is that your software won't be right on the first cut. The good news is that you can get it right. This is where the importance of *testing and iteration* come in. Testing helps you measure where you are, as you refine the design and the code to get closer and closer to the objective. It's a simple enough concept, but you have to actually do it.

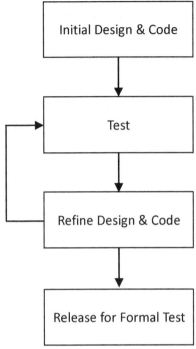

Test, Refine, and Iterate

Your tests must sufficiently exercise what you've written, or you can't really be sure it's right. For this reason, testability should be a major consideration in your design work. Consider writing the tests before you even write your implementation code. A *test-first approach* helps you think through design details. Whether you write the code first or the tests first, the tests need to be comprehensive. Test as many of the elements in your requirements as possible. Test not only the primary path of a feature, but its variations.

Iteration means returning back to your work and improving it. You must test and refine over and over, until it is finally correct and complete. It's right here that many developers fall short: they stop iterating because they are out of time, or are tired, or haven't tested sufficiently. Don't break out of the loop early: you need to bring your code to completion, and should budget sufficient time for this necessary work in your estimates.

---

*Iteratively test and refine your design and code until
it is correct, complete, and clean. See it through.*

Practice Continuous Improvement

So then, to create quality software we must be realistic and accept that iterations of testing and refinement are necessary activities in order to get code right. Nevertheless, we should also strive to get better at our first cut of the code, because iterations take time and we would like to have as few of them as possible. To achieve this means dedicating yourself to *continuous improvement*, where you are ever-learning and ever-improving the software.

Are you a better programmer than you were a year ago? A month ago? A week ago? For the developer who practices continuous improvement, the answer is always yes. If you aren't learning something new constantly, you won't be nearly as effective in improving the quality of your software. The code will improve as you improve.

Become a student of good design and development techniques. You can't apply the right approach or pattern if you've never learned it. You can learn from many sources, including books, online training courses, web sites, and fellow developers. Not everyone's guidance is correct guidance, so carefully consider the sources of your information.

Similarly, learn more about the languages, tools, libraries, and products you use until you are fully proficient. An insufficient knowledge of your programming tools leads to problematic code and nasty surprises. For example, there are plenty of programmers out there working in JavaScript who don't understand the difference between == and ===, or are unaware that the month parameter of the Date constructor is zero-based. These are things you don't want to learn the hard way.

Learn from others on your team, and teach things to others on your team. If you and your fellow developers never have technical discussions, you're failing to sharpen each other and your team may have an uneven baseline of skills. Take the initiative and start sharing.

Learn from your mistakes and successes. Take a moment to analyze why something turned out the way it did. Change your work habits accordingly.

Learn from your bugs. Each time you fix an issue, that's a learning opportunity. If you find yourself repeating the same kinds of bugs, that's a clear indication of a knowledge gap or a bad habit.

Best of all, you can learn a great deal from developing. Apply what you've learned in a project at the next opportunity. When you're trying something new, take steps to avoid risk such as asking for a buddy code review from a knowledgeable developer.

Commit to Continuous Improvement and keep raising the quality of your code.

Finish the Work

Getting your designs and implementation code right usually requires iteration, in which you refine and refactor your work repeatedly until it is truly right. This is the point where many developers fail to follow through, deciding things are good enough and moving on before they have really finished. When quality is the objective, good enough really isn't good enough. Don't leave that overly long function in place. Don't fail to refactor that not-quite-right class. Don't skip the clean-up and commenting of your code. Write those unit tests.

Finish the work. Don't settle for good enough.

Many development teams have the concept of a "Definition of Done", which is a checklist of all the things that need to be true before a developer can declare work complete. A Definition of Done is a good and useful thing, but all too often it ends up being guidance that is given but not enforced. If your team doesn't have a Definition of Done, work to get one put in place. If your team doesn't enforce its Definition of Done, suggest reviews when a developer declares completion. In the review, each item in the Definition of Done should be verified.

☐ **Checked against requirements**
The work has been checked against the requirements/stories. All Conditions of Acceptance have been satisfied.

☐ **User Experience correct**
The user interface, styling, and interactions match the story's visual artifacts and wireframes.

☐ **Tasks Up-to-Date**
If you track development tasks, update the progress of completed tasks. If there is code debt, ensure it is reflected in development tasks.

☐ **Code Complete**
Code is solid, well-structured and commented. Dead code has been removed. Error handling is in place.

☐ **Optimized**
Performance requirements met. Web pages score an acceptable grade in web page performance tools. Caching strategy in place. Database tables are properly indexed.

☐ **Localized**
Localization is in place. The code has been tested in multiple locales and languages.

☐ **Tested**
The developer has tested the code. Unit tests have been created and are all passing. Obvious bugs have been found and fixed.

☐ **Reviewed**
The code has been checked with code analysis tools and reviewed by a fellow developer.

☐ **Checked in**
The code has been checked in to source control.

Sample Definition of Done

If you're thinking all of this amounts to a lot of time, you're absolutely correct. However, far more time is wasted when these things aren't done due to the bugs that result.

More Quality in Your Design

Think Big, then Think Small

When you're designing and implementing software, it's helpful to first think big and then think small.

Start with the big picture: the entities and business logic in the requirements should be clearly reflected in the design of your interfaces, classes, and services. The way these constructs are able to interact should strongly match how entities interact in the requirements. In other words, both your code and the requirements should convey the same model. If the macro structure of your code bears little resemblance to the patterns in the requirements, you're already on the road to problems: refactor until the code embodies the model. Design unit tests and integration tests that will prove the code correctly implements the model.

Then, think small: as you write the implementation code, don't get too ambitious. Developers get into trouble when the code they write is too complex or clever or just plain too long. Write small, targeted units of code that are so simple you can be easily confident in their correctness. Your code should be boringly straightforward and a joy to maintain. Make the code complete and clean and crisp. Structure it well and comment it. Write unit tests and integration tests to prove everything works.

Think big, reflecting the model in your design; then think small, writing maintainable units of code.

41

Put the Correct Walls in Place

Software is, well, *soft*. Without imposing structure, you can do anything—and that's dangerous. With structure we can have software layers with protective boundaries, and safe containers for implementation code that puts constraints on what the code can do. Architecture and top-level design are both activities that deliberately put up walls. Done correctly, those walls are highly valuable and necessary because they force software components to coordinate in a valid way. Done improperly, those walls (or their lack) can make it impossible to implement correctly or permit problems to creep into the code that could have been avoided.

Your architecture should embody the nature of what you're building. If you were inspecting the blueprints for a house, you'd likely be able to tell it was a house, because you'd see things intrinsic to a house such as a living room, kitchen, and bedrooms. Likewise, the blueprints for an office building or a theater clearly communicate what they are. The same thing should be true of your software architecture: when someone inspects the architecture of your resort property management software, the top level arrangement and interfaces should strongly convey resort property management—not PHP or ASP.NET or whatever technologies you're using.

Arrange your architecture with proper boundaries
and interfaces that reinforce the nature of what
you're building.

Use Proven Patterns and Techniques

Few software problems are new, so there's little reason to start from scratch when there's so much good guidance available—much of it free and online. When you're venturing into new territory in a software problem, take the time to check whether there is a known good pattern or technique you can apply. Given how much work goes into getting software right, finding an already-proven pattern is tremendously valuable.

Don't reinvent the wheel—unless you really need a different kind of wheel, or have reason to believe you can make a better wheel.

This doesn't mean using patterns just for the sake of using patterns, nor should you adopt a pattern if it's a poor fit for the problem you're trying to solve.

Don't reinvent the wheel unless you have a good reason for it. When there is a proven pattern or technique available that fits your problem well, use it.

Separation of Concerns and Single Responsibility

Separation of Concerns (SoC) is a principle for separating functionality into distinct areas to handle each concern with as little overlap as possible. A "concern" can be any abstraction that is relevant to the problem you are trying to solve, such as a business entity, a feature, or a behavior. This fundamental concept underlies many software engineering methodologies and best practices. It helps us manage complexity.

Having separate classes for your business entities is an obvious use for SoC. If your requirements discuss customers, orders, and products you could represent those concerns in Customer, Order, and Product classes. Another example of SoC is web pages, which use HTML for organizing content, CSS for declarative styling, and JavaScript for procedural code that provides behavior and interaction. Yet another example is the Model-View-Controller pattern.

Separate concerns into distinct areas.

SoC is closely related to another concept, the Single Responsibility Principle (SRP): A class or module should have one and only one responsibility, and be the only thing with that responsibility.

When the description of a class or method includes the word "and", that's a tip off that SRP is being violated. For example, if you had a Utilities class that logs events and also does time zone conversion, there are multiple responsibilities because those functions have nothing to do with each other. It would be better to separate these functions into an EventLog class and a TimeZone class. Code with multiple responsibilities is difficult to unit test, because you can't isolate each responsibility.

One thing to watch out for over time is responsibility creep: classes that initially have single responsibilities sometimes get extended over time and end up having multiple responsibilities. When you see this happen, it's time to refactor back to a clean separation of responsibilities.

Design classes or modules to have a singular purpose.

Cohesion and Coupling

Cohesion refers to the functionality a component provides. High (good) cohesion means what's in the class contributes to the type the object is meant to represent. Low cohesion means the class contains functionality that doesn't belong together. For example, an Invoice class that encapsulates all of the functionality needed for invoices has high cohesion; a BusinessDocument class that combines order, invoice, contract, and statement functionality has low cohesion. Components with a single purpose tend to have high cohesion: a focused class is a cohesive class.

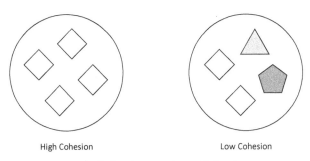

High Cohesion   Low Cohesion

High Cohesion vs. Low Cohesion

Coupling is how dependent software components are upon each other. If you have an Order class that has an instance of an Address class, there is coupling between them. If Order works with an instance of IAddress instead of Address, the coupling is looser.

Two software components are loosely-coupled if changes to one rarely require changes to the other. Coupling is necessary in order for objects to work together, but loose coupling is desirable because it allows objects to be updated with little to no impact on other objects. Loose coupling is an example of the Law of Demeter (LoD), which states that each unit of software should only have a limited knowledge of others, and "should only talk to friends."

With tightly-coupled objects, things are quite different: changes cause ripples of other changes, which compromises maintainability and quality. You typically have to understand all the parts well in order to make a change; with loose coupling, you don't.

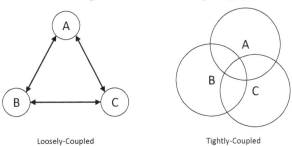

Loosely-Coupled   Tightly-Coupled

Loose Coupling vs. Tight Coupling

What you want, then, is *high cohesion within modules* and *loose coupling between modules*. In the diagram below, look how complex and tangled the low cohesion, tightly-coupled solution on the left is. Now compare it to the highly cohesive, loosely-coupled solution on the right, which has a clean separation of concerns and is sure to have much simpler code—strongly improving quality and maintainability.

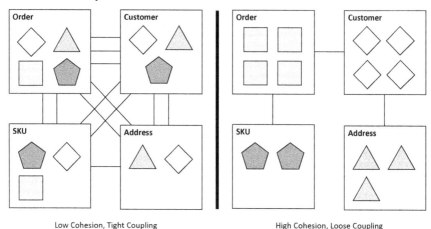

Low Cohesion, Tight Coupling   High Cohesion, Loose Coupling

The Difference Proper Cohesion and Coupling Make

Strive for High Cohesion within modules and Loose Coupling between modules.

It's a mistake to consider coupling or cohesion in isolation when making design decisions. You sometimes have to make trade-offs between coupling, cohesion, and other software engineering principles. For example, a single class that is highly cohesive may also be complex; if you choose to refactor the complex class into several simpler classes, you reduce complexity but at the cost of lower cohesiveness and tighter coupling.

Handle Exceptions Intentionally

When code encounters an error, we expect the error to be handled. Every one of us has experienced the ugliness that results when an error isn't handled by any layer of an application and it gives up the ghost. In most modern development environments, the majority of errors surface as exceptions.

Therefore, you definitely want comprehensive exception handling throughout your application. However, that doesn't mean every single function you write needs a try-catch. Nor should you be "eating exceptions", where every single error is trapped in the function that caught it and disregarded.

The correct way to handle errors is intentional exception handling. For any unit of code, there should always be a *designated responsible party* who will handle an exception. That might be the immediate function, but if the error cannot be handled gracefully it should be allowed to bubble up. A layer of code higher up the call chain may have better context for handling the error. However, it needs to be dealt with somewhere—if nowhere else, at the top boundary layer of the software.

Handling an exception can mean a number of things. In try-catch blocks, catch *specific* types of exceptions you anticipate—for example a database exception. If the type of exception is one that was anticipated—such as a database error—you can plan an appropriate response. That could mean returning a particular value to the caller; retrying an operation (but be sure you do not end up in an endless retry situation); or letting the exception be handled by the caller. You may want to log the exception detail so you can be aware the error occurred and have the information needed to study it.

Avoid catching *all* exceptions: this means you don't really know the state of your application or whether it is safe to continue running. However, one place exceptions should be firmly trapped is at boundary layers. For example, a service or API will typically have a response that communicates success or failure with error details rather than throwing an exception.

Design intentional exception handling into your application.

More Quality in Your Code

An elegant design means little if it is poorly implemented. Quality code is code that is clean, understandable, well-factored, and proven; not an unfinished mess. I like Kent Beck's 4 Rules of Simple Design, which I'll express this way:

1. Proven: you have tests for your code, and they all pass.
2. Understandable: the intention of your code is clear (to others, not just you).
3. Well-factored: follows the Don't Repeat Yourself rule.
4. Small: your code is clean and simple, free of the unnecessary.

You often recognize code like this when you encounter it. Go and do likewise.

Code for an Audience

Just because you've gotten your code to function correctly does not mean your code is a model citizen. There will come a time when others have to understand your code and change it. Will they be able to easily understand your code in a short time, or will it be a riddle they endlessly puzzle over? Will modifying your code be a simple matter, or a leap into the unknown?

When your code is incomprehensible or difficult to maintain, all you've done is created a kind of time bomb: you've sown the seeds of future bugs which will arise when developers eventually have to modify your unfathomable code.

You should always code for an audience. Write code with the expectation it will be reviewed, and if that's not an actual expectation, you yourself should schedule a review. Your code needs to:

- …be easy to read and well-commented.
- …be readily understandable, not an enigma.
- …have intuitive and helpful names for variables, classes, functions, and services.
- …not have surprise behaviors or side effects.
- …be clean and well-structured.

Code for an audience. Write readable, maintainable code that others can quickly understand and modify with minimal ramp-up or danger.

Don't Repeat Yourself

Duplicate code is wasteful: it needlessly increases the size and complexity of your code and causes maintenance headaches. When a developer uses copy and paste to duplicate code, that shortcut weakens the quality of your application. Instead, you should recognize the opportunity to create a well-known object and re-use it.

Imagine you have written code to insert a task record in your database. Later on, you have other tasks to create and copy that original code in a few other places. You now have multiple instances of code that do the same thing. Some time goes by, and you make some changes to the first instance of task code. Another developer changes one of the code instances to fix a bug. Now you have several different variations of that code, plus a brewing maintenance problem. A better approach would have been to create a task class containing the task creation code and use the class whenever you need to add a task or perform other operations on tasks. That's the principle of Don't Repeat Yourself: avoid duplication by coding something once, then reusing it.

The DRY principle, as formulated by Andy Hunt and Dave Thomas in *The Pragmatic Programmer*, states "every piece of knowledge must have a single, unambiguous, authoritative representation within a system." This can be applied to many things in software, including classes, functions, markup, styles, database schema, and scripts. Have *one* class that handles a contact; have *one* markup view that displays a confirmation prompt; have *one* style for a dialog title. You could say that the opposite of DRY is WET (Write Everything Twice, or We Enjoy Typing). DRY and class inheritance combine well.

Don't Repeat Yourself. Implement logic once in a well-known object and re-use it.

Avoid Complex Code

Complex code is a major source of bugs, which means you should studiously avoid it; think of complex code as unfinished code. All complex code can be simplified into smaller units with refactoring. As you refactor, be sure to also avoid complexity in how those smaller units integrate, or you've only moved complexity from place to another. Once again, this means iteration and following through until the end result is satisfactory.

Human beings lack the capacity to keep all the details of complex code in their heads, which is why it's so important to logically divide functionality into smaller, more manageable pieces. Sometimes, though, developers don't do this sufficiently and take on too much at a time. When this happens, the code can get out of control. Even the developer who wrote the code may have difficulty understanding it a year later.

Refactor complex code until it is no longer complex.

Write Less Code

The less code you write, the fewer bugs you will have. This is not meant in a humorous way, it's a simple fact. Each new unit of code you write is like a new child; it will need care and maintenance for the rest of its life. The fewer mouths to feed, the better. It's hard to believe there was a time when programmer productivity was measured in lines of code written. That's not only a useless metric, it's backwards.

Therefore, don't write code that isn't needed. If you must write a unit of code, make it efficient. Don't take a page of code for something that could be accomplished in a few lines—that is, if the few lines work just as well and are not cryptic or unclear;

changes that make your code less readable and understandable should be avoided.

Developers write unnecessary code when:
- They write functionality that already exists in a library.
- They copy and paste existing code.
- They write code that already exists elsewhere in the application.
- Their algorithm is inefficient.
- They fail to refactor.
- They fall into the trap of "gold plating" their software by adding features nobody asked for.

Write as much code as necessary while bringing your implementation to life—but once you have it working and debugged, strive for brevity in your end result.

Avoid Code Bloat: Less is More.

Have the Courage to Refactor or Rewrite

Refactoring can sometimes be a lot of work, but it's a straightforward activity if you're in the habit of doing it regularly rather than occasionally. When it's necessary you shouldn't shirk from it. Code that is complex or difficult to maintain should be refactored without hesitation.

There are times when it becomes clear that a section of code isn't ever going to function correctly unless you take drastic measures. Rewriting is never something to take lightly, but sometimes nothing will save the patient except a transplant. If you are convinced you need to rewrite a large section of code, it can be useful to refactor it first, because you may only need to replace a smaller unit of code after doing so.

With refactoring and especially with rewriting, there can be a worry that the exercise will upset existing functionality. The best way to guard against that is to have good test coverage before you start, then work incrementally. Use the tests as checkpoints to verify each round of changes hasn't had some adverse effect on the behavior of the code.

Comment Responsibly

If you've ever had to work on a piece of code you didn't understand, you can appreciate that a few comments might have made a big difference in reducing the amount of time it took to understand what was going on. But you can also appreciate that if the code had been structured differently, it might have been readily understandable without comments.

There are all sorts of opinions out there about code comments. Some feel you need to comment code heavily. Others say code should have no comments, because the code should be written so well its meaning is clear. Unless you're a brand-new programmer, you've probably encountered examples of both practices—and found them extreme at times.

In the example below, the comments are too much. The pertinent information could be explained in one line rather than fifteen. The edit history would be better recorded in source control. On the other hand, if there were no comments at all the purpose of the function might be unclear to some readers.

```
// ****************
// *              *
// *   SqlString  *
// *              *
// ****************
// Purpose: Return a version of a string suitable for inclu-
sion in a SQL query.
//
// Inputs: text ......... string to be included in a SQL
query. Example: O'Leary
//
// Outputs: <result> ..... string with apostrophe character
"escaped". Example: O''Leary
//
// Edit History:
// 01-15-14 by KLZ. Created.
// 01-17-14 by KLZ. Simplified code.
```

```
// 04-22-15 by NJ. Added null and empty string checking.

public String SqlString(String text)
{
    if (!String.IsNullOrEmpty(text))
    {
        text = text.Replace("'", "''");
    }
    return text;
}
```

Comment overkill

Arbitrary rules about how many comments to have seems like a bad idea. A much better rule of thumb is that comments should explain the *purpose* of the code and anything the reader needs to know that wouldn't be obvious. Include comments where they communicate something important. If you can communicate that same message in your code, that's great. When you can't, include a comment. Have you ever written a particularly significant line of code and wished you could end it in an exclamation point? That's the time to add a comment.

Write clean code that communicates most of what the reader needs to know. Add a comment to major sections of code, public interfaces, and whenever you need to tell the reader something important.

Here are some good guidelines for commenting:
1. Write your code with the intent that comments won't be necessary. Strive for meaningful names and avoid cryptic code.
2. Preface major sections of code such as a class, function or group of style rules with a comment explaining its purpose.

3. When there is an unusual pattern of code that repeats, comment the first one as an explanation. For example, you might explain the order of values in a data list.
4. Assume the reader of your code and comments is not yourself.
5. Tell the reader what they need to know. When you must have code that exists for an unusual reason or has effects that might not be anticipated, comments can be extraordinarily helpful.
6. Comment public interfaces. Formal boundaries, such as an API or service, deserve to be well-described. If your development tools can generate documentation from comments, that's an additional reason to have them.
7. When you update code, make sure the comments for the code are still correct. Out-of-date comments that misinform the reader are even worse than no comments.
8. Remember to remove "temporary comments", which you might have written while you were getting the code right or debugging a problem.

Practice Defensive Programming

Like defensive driving, *defensive programming* is about not making assumptions and handling the unexpected. For example:
- A function should have explicit checks whether any of its parameters are null.
- Numeric values should not be assumed to be in a valid range.
- User input should not be assumed to be valid.
- A switch statement should include a default case to handle the unexpected.
- Code should anticipate invalid values from functions and handle it intelligently.
- Code should anticipate that anything it calls might result in an exception or error, and handle it intelligently.

This is especially important in modern development, where so much of the code you interact with isn't your code. Every time you add third-party code to your solution, you are introducing more unknowns.

Let's consider an example. Jim has written the C# function below to retrieve a customer's latest statement and display it:

```
void ShowLatestStatement(String customerId)
{
    DisplayStatement(GetLatestStatement(customerId));
}
```

This code may happen to work when Jim runs it, but it isn't hardened. What happens if the customerId is invalid, or there is no customer with that Id? GetLatestStatement, if it doesn't throw an exception, will likely return a value the DisplayStatement function will not know what to do with. Even if the customerId is for an existing customer, what does GetLatestStatement return for a new customer who has no statements? It is likely DisplayStatement will be in for a surprise and will fail.

A defensive version of this function is shown below that checks for nulls. While this is quite a bit longer than the original, it will hold up to abuse.

```
void ShowLatestStatement(String customerId)
{
    if (customerId != null)
    {
        Statement statement = GetLatestStatement(customerId);
        if (statement != null)
        {
            DisplayStatement(statement);
        }
    }
}
```

Other defenses could be added as well, such as handling exceptions thrown by GetLatestStatement or DisplayStatement. Then again, the developer might choose to have the caller handle exceptions instead of ShowLatestStatement. Defensive programming is important, but it needs to be done carefully: too much of it can add unnecessary complexity or hide errors that should be surfaced.

Avoid assumptions and anticipate the unexpected.
Harden your code using Defensive Programming
techniques.

Scope Carefully

Scope determines the visibility of variables and their lifetime. Improperly scoped variables can result in surprise values or keeping values in memory longer than necessary; this is especially true of global variables, which frequently don't need to be global.

Scoping is a frequent problem in JavaScript. It's easy to assign a variable without remembering the *var* statement, resulting in a global variable that you might have thought was local. The x = 5 statement in the function below results in x being a global variable.

```
function y() {
    x = 5;
}
```

Many developers are also unaware that JavaScript does not scope variables defined with *var* to code blocks—rather, they are hoisted to the scope of the function. For example, consider the JavaScript code below. You might reason the variable z should not exist by the time the console.log(z) statement executes—but it does, because JavaScript hoists the declaration of z to the top of function y. Surprise!

```
var x = 1;
function y() {
    if (x === 1) {
        var z = 'David ';
    }
    console.log(z);
}
```

> *Minimize global variables. Scope variables appropriately based on where they are needed.*

Scoping can also refer to selectors, such as CSS style rules or jQuery selectors. Overly-broad selectors are a common problem and lead to unwanted side effects. If you've ever made a style rule change only to later discover it unexpectedly affected other parts of the application, a rule's overly-broad selector may be the culprit.

Use Code Analysis Tools

Many languages and development tools have code analysis tools available. You can and should use these tools to discover code problems: code that conforms to standards and follows accepted practices has better quality. Typically these tools perform static code analysis, where source code is scanned and checked against a set of rules, producing a list of warnings.

Using these tools can be very humbling, but is definitely worthwhile. When you take a listing of code you thought was perfect and receive a bunch of warnings from an analysis tool, you'll likely learn something new about the language you're working in and what the best patterns are. Use what you learn to improve your coding habits.

Code analysis tools exist to bring issues or potential issues to your attention. That doesn't mean every issue necessarily has to be addressed or is of equal importance, so make intelligent decisions about taking remedial action. Developers sometimes struggle with analysis tools because they take issue with one or more of the rules. When you're in that situation, read up on what the rule means and why it exists. If you still disagree with the rule, check whether the code analysis tool allows you to exclude rules or add new rules. If so, you can customize the analysis. Before excluding a rule, though, be sure you have a good reason for not applying it.

---

*Use code analysis tools regularly and keep your code
in compliance with standards.*

Let's look at a few examples of these tools.

Example: csslint

Front-end web developers can use the *csslint* tool to analyze CSS style rules. csslint checks rule syntax for correctness and applies a set of rules to detect poor patterns and inefficient rules.

892	14	Disallow units for 0 values	Values of 0 shouldn't have units specified: `padding: 0px 20px;`	All
895	5	Disallow adjoining classes	Don't use adjoining classes: `.form-group.recruiter-input .control-label {`	IE6
899	5	Disallow adjoining classes	Don't use adjoining classes: `.form-group.recruiter-input .control-label, .card-buttons.`	IE6
910	5	Beware of broken box size	Using height with border can sometimes make elements larger than you expect: `border: 4px dashed #eaeaea;`	All
910	5	Beware of broken box size	Using width with border can sometimes make elements larger than you expect: `border: 4px dashed #eaeaea;`	All
911	5	Disallow !important	Use of !important: `border-radius: 75px !important;`	All
913	5	Disallow duplicate properties	Duplicate property 'color' found: `color: #eaeaea;`	All
914	5	Disallow duplicate properties	Duplicate property 'font-weight' found: `font-weight: normal;`	All
920	19	Disallow units for 0 values	Values of 0 shouldn't have units specified: `margin: -75px 0px 0px -75px;`	All
920	23	Disallow units for 0 values	Values of 0 shouldn't have units specified: `margin: -75px 0px 0px -75px;`	All
920	5	Disallow duplicate properties	Duplicate property 'margin' found: `margin: -75px 0px 0px -75px;`	All
924	9	Disallow !important	Use of !important: `font-size: 36px !important;`	All
934	5	Beware of broken box size	Using width with border can sometimes make elements larger than you expect: `border: 2px solid #3f64ac;`	All

csslint analysis of CSS style rules

Example: jslint

JavaScript code can be analyzed with jslint, a code quality analysis tool developed by Douglas Crockford. jslint targets a professional subset of JavaScript and identifies code in violation of its rules.

jslint analysis of JavaScript code

Example: FxCop

Microsoft.NET developers can use the FxCop tool (short for "framework cop") which is integrated into Visual Studio. FxCop scans .NET object code (such as compiled C# code) and reports violations of the .NET Framework guidelines, including security issues.

FxCop analysis of C# .NET code

Profile and Optimize

Your code not only needs to work correctly, it also needs to be efficient. Profile your code, then optimize it based on the findings.

Leverage Profiling Tools

Depending on the tier of your solution and your development platform, you may have profiling tools available; if you do, use them. They can provide invaluable insights into where bottlenecks are. There are profiling tools for databases, servers, programming languages, CSS, web pages, and cloud services.

Database profiling tools can show you which queries or stored procedures are taking the longest, or point out where adding an index to a table would benefit query time.

Web developers can take advantage of free tools to profile their pages. For example, Yahoo's free YSlow tool, shown below, is a popular profiling tool for web pages. It grades pages in many areas such as the number of HTTP requests and whether JavaScript and CSS files are minified. This kind of analysis gives you a ready-made attack list for improving performance.

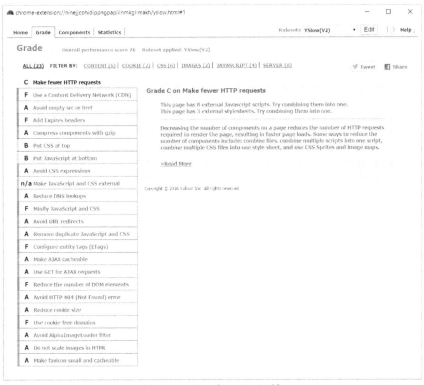

Web Page Grading in YSlow

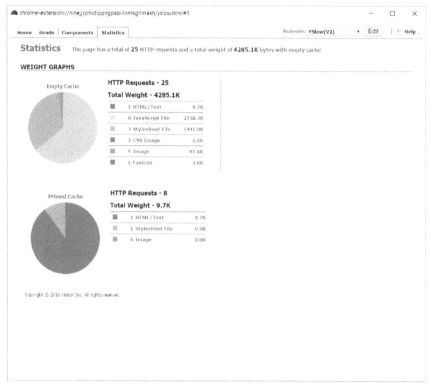

HTTP Request Statistics in YSlow

When no profiling tool is available for a layer of your software, consider whether you can do your own profiling. A simple mechanism such as writing checkpoint messages to a log can be enough to reveal where bottlenecks are.

Leverage profiling tools to discover opportunities for optimization.

Look for Inefficiencies in Your Code

In addition to using profiling tools, you and your fellow developers should regularly be reviewing each other's code and looking for opportunities to optimize. To this day, I am amazed at how much inefficient code can be found just by taking the time to examine code. When developers are in a hurry, they fail to realize they are doing unnecessary activities, or repeating activities more times than necessary, or failing to leverage mechanisms like caching.

Here's a real life example of an inefficiency I found years back. A young developer on my team had written a code loop in this pattern, intended to reset the balance field of every student record to $0.00.

```
for each student record
{
    Read the record
    If balance > 0.00
    {
        balance = 0.00
    }
    Write the record
}
```

An inefficient update loop

The problem with this code is that it rewrites every record regardless of whether it changed or not. It does unnecessary disk writes, and unnecessary I/O is bad for performance. It works, but it isn't efficient. The simple correction is to only do the write if the balance needs to be reset.

```
for each student record
{
    Read the record
    If balance > 0.00
    {
        balance = 0.00
        Write the record
    }
}
```

```
}
```

A more efficient update loop

Getting a buddy review of your code is recommended, because we sometimes have blind spots that prevent us from seeing problems in our own code.

Review your code for inefficiencies.

Fix Broken Windows

The broken windows theory states that in a neighborhood that is not maintained, deterioration will escalate. For example, if there is a broken window that doesn't get fixed, it's only a matter of time before other windows will be broken and more serious vandalism will follow. By not keeping the neighborhood maintained, a signal has been sent: "we don't care what happens here." Now contrast that to what you feel when you enter a place that is orderly, clean, and beautifully maintained: everyone treats it with respect.

The same thing can happen in software, where a "broken window" can mean such things as a flawed design, badly written code, a sloppy UI, or a security hole. If parts of the application code are a mess and it is left that way, others working on the code may continue the sloppiness and pick up bad practices. Tolerating code in this condition leads to a lowering of standards which compromises quality. Developers need to care about the maintainability of the code and fix a broken window whenever one is encountered. Regular code reviews and scans with code analysis tools can help find them, but it's the "fix it on the spot" mentality whenever you find a broken window that results in proper upkeep.

Don't let broken windows shatter the orderliness of your code: fix them, and keep the neighborhood clean.

Fix broken windows. Keep the neighborhood clean.

Remove Debugging Code and Dead Code

After getting your code working and debugged, you may have left a trail of rubble behind in the form of debugging code. That can include JavaScript debugger statements and console.log statements; server-side logging of information that is no longer needed; and extra display information that was added as a debugging aid.

Dead code means commented out sections of code, and these should likewise be removed when you are finalizing your work.

Manage Code Debt

Code debt refers to work you know you need to do but are putting off to the future. If you've implemented 6 out of 8 COAs in a story, the remainder is code debt. If you know you still need to add error handling to that function, that's code debt.

The best way to deal with code debt, of course, is to not have any—if you can possibly take care of that remaining item now instead of later you should do so. When we defer things, they sometimes never get done.

When code debt is unavoidable, there are some things you can do to manage it:

- Put a reminder in the code, such as a // TODO: comment. If you standardize on a common prefix like "TODO:", you can search for it, giving you an easy way to find all of the To Do comments in the code.
- If you track development tasks in a tool, be sure the task is being tracked.
- If appropriate, write a placeholder or "stub" function, perhaps with some Band-Aid code, which you will replace with the real code.

In the listing below, the developer does not have time to write a student ranking function but the rest of the code needs one. A placeholder function is put in the place with a TODO comment, to be eventually replaced with an implementation.

```
// Rank the student based on GPA
public int rank(String studentId)
{
    // TODO: look up student GPA and compute a ranking
    //       in the meantime, return a hard-coded rank.

    return 90;
}
```

Don't put things off. If code debt is unavoidable,
manage it with placeholder code and task tracking.

PART II: DEVELOPER TESTING

"Testing is not a phase, it's a way of life." —Elisabeth
Hendrickson

Developers spend too little time testing and know too little about testing. In order to achieve high-quality software, you need to become a proficient tester.

Chapter 3 describes how to test your own work comprehensively before handing it off for formal test.

Chapter 4 covers Functional Testing, where you confirm your work satisfies requirements.

Chapter 5 covers Hostile Testing, where you employ different techniques to try to break the software.

Chapter 6 is about Automated Testing.

Chapter 7 is about Analyzing and Debugging issues.

3 TESTING YOUR OWN WORK

"A true professional does not waste the time and money of other people by handing over software that is not reasonably free of obvious bugs; that has not undergone minimal unit testing; that does not meet the specifications and requirements; that is gold-plated with unnecessary features; or that looks like junk."–Daniel Read

Narrative

Jon next met up with Jai, one of the testers in the QA group. Jon asked, "Our team really seems to know what it is doing when it comes to quality. I've talked to some of my fellow developers, but I wanted to get your opinion on why that is?" Jai thought for a moment, then responded, "It is a lot better now but it wasn't always that way. I'd like to take credit for it, but to be honest I think much of the shift in quality has come from the developers: they have really committed to being part of the quality process instead of just reacting to it."

"And how has that made things different for you?" asked Jon. "Well," said Jai, "It used to be very easy to find bugs in the solution. When we would get a new build, we would find dozens of bugs our very first day with it. But that has all changed. The developers find the obvious bugs and fix them before they release software to us. As a result, we have to work much harder to find issues."

"That almost sounds like it has made a problem for you." said Jon. "Maybe management will conclude the developers are doing such as great job on quality that the QA group isn't necessary?" Jai smiled. "Oh, there's no danger of that." He pointed to a poster on the wall that read, "'If you do your job, I can do mine.'" Jai continued, "We are now able to focus on what we should have been doing all along: exhaustive testing, finding the subtle issues, and making sure we have good coverage with our automated tests.

"We do some kinds of testing the developers don't do, such as UI automation tests, performance tests, and security audits. It was hard to get all those things done previously because we had our hands full just cataloging all the bugs we found in each build. Now that the developers also build automated tests, this gives us a great starting point for QA's own tests. The software has also become easier to write tests for as a result."

Developer Testing

In the entire history of software development, the number of software projects that have had sufficient time and resource for testing is extremely small (some would say the number is zero). Your project is in the same boat, which makes it essential that you do your part in the testing effort.

There are some differences between a developer testing their own work and what QA does: the idea is not for you to simply duplicate the same tests QA would perform. For one thing, QA has more time available for testing than you do since you also have development work to do. Rather, you are striving to shake out the obvious problems. QA should be laboring to find the subtle, harder-to-find problems.

Another difference is that you the developer have a knowledge of how the code works, which inherently makes your testing *white box testing*. You can devise tests that will exercise different code paths. In contrast, QA is typically performing *black box testing* that is based on requirements without a knowledge of the internal implementation.

Test Until Free of Obvious Bugs

Most developers don't do enough testing, turning software over to QA before it is reasonably solid. All that results in is a large bug count, because QA is rapidly finding obvious problems that the developer should have found in the first place. Instead, don't turn software over for formal testing until it is free of obvious bugs.

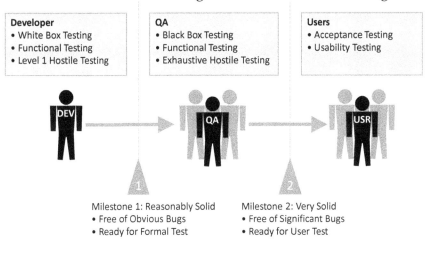

Developer	QA	Users
• White Box Testing	• Black Box Testing	• Acceptance Testing
• Functional Testing	• Functional Testing	• Usability Testing
• Level 1 Hostile Testing	• Exhaustive Hostile Testing	

Milestone 1: Reasonably Solid
• Free of Obvious Bugs
• Ready for Formal Test

Milestone 2: Very Solid
• Free of Significant Bugs
• Ready for User Test

Don't turn in your work for formal testing until it is reasonably solid and free of obvious bugs.

If you are finding you don't have enough time for testing, then you should change how you estimate to factor in test time. This may require some bravery on your part, because most projects move into a stage where there is significant deadline pressure. Taking on less work in a development cycle to allow adequate testing time may not be popular, but it is far preferable to turning in buggy software. Turning in buggy software will only lead to a snowballing bug count that will fail to make anyone happy. Stand firm.

To be sure, more is needed beyond your own efforts and that's why it's also necessary to have other people involved in testing: quality assurance departments and user acceptance testing will try things that will never occur to you. The purpose of your self-testing is to shake out the obvious and deliver a very solid starting point for formal testing.

Types of Testing

There are many kinds of testing, and quite a few ways to categorize testing approaches. Here are some common ones you should be acquainted with. Note some kinds of testing fall into more than one category.

Functional Testing: Start Here

You should perform multiple types of testing, but the one you should always start with is functional testing, described in Chapter 4. This simply means ensuring the software does what it is supposed to when used properly. Here you are not trying to trick the application with poor input or unexpected patterns of use: you want to verify that a competent user, using the software as intended, is able to perform their business tasks successfully.

Functional Testing is also known as *Positive Use Case Testing*. The objective is to confirm that the requirements are fully satisfied, including all conditions of acceptance. Good coverage is essential here: don't overlook any conditions of acceptance in your stories.

There's an important reason why you should do this type of testing first. If your code can't hold up to a positive use case test, there's no point in doing any hostile testing. Failure to handle positive use case testing can indicate that you may have missed or misunderstood some of the requirements, have an incorrect technical design, or have a flawed code implementation.

If positive use case testing fails, you're not as done as you thought you were! You need to go back to the requirements and your code and get it right. Then return to testing.

Test the positive use case first.

While you're doing your functional testing is an excellent time to capture some screen shots and document the steps you are performing. You can use that to create a walk-through or release notes when you pass the software to QA for formal testing.

If positive use case testing doesn't reveal any issues, you have a tentatively correct core implementation—but is it hardened against the abuse that it will encounter in the real world? That's where hostile testing comes in.

Hostile Testing

Hostile Testing, described in Chapter 5, attempts to cause failures through improper or unexpected use. The majority of testing techniques are hostile testing, so there are many types to choose from. Here are some examples:

- Trying to bypass input field validation
- Trying to make a calculation divide by zero
- Trying to break a business rule
- Trying to bypass security defenses
- Trying to inject dangerous SQL scripts in an input field

White Box and Black Box Testing

White Box Testing is testing influenced by a knowledge of the internal implementation. The opposite of white box testing is Black Box Testing, which is based on requirements or what a user might do, without any knowledge of internals. This may lead you to believe that developers do white box testing and QA testers do black box testing, but it's actually the type of testing that determines this.

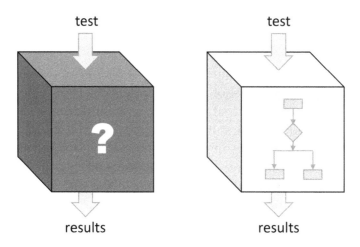

Black Box and White Box Testing

White box testing includes unit testing and integration testing. The design of tests and the testing process is informed by the structure of the solution code. Here are some examples of white box testing:

- Creating a test for each method of a class.
- Creating a test for each server action.
- Testing each path of a switch statement in a function.
- Testing each parameter variation of a database stored procedure.

Black box testing includes functional testing, usability testing, and user acceptance testing. The design of tests and the test process is based on requirements, documentation, or ad-hoc exploration. Here are some examples of black box testing:

- Testing that a story's conditions of acceptance are satisfied

- Following a procedure described in the documentation
- Attempting to perform a business task
- Exploring the software as one of the target personas

Unit, Integration, and System Testing

Developers have been taught for years about 3 levels of testing: *unit testing* tests a single software component; *integration testing* tests a combination of components; and *system testing* tests the entire solution, also called *end-to-end testing*. A nice simple concept, like Russian nesting dolls.

These distinctions are useful but they are also vague and sometimes misapplied, so let's get specific. Developers are often told they'd better have unit tests, but what exactly is a "unit" in your project? does unit testing refer to individual functions or individual classes or individual service methods? This lack of specificity is understandable, since applications vary in size and complexity, languages and platforms vary in organization, and technology changes over time.

The key point to all of this is that you and your team will need to decide what the logical unit of testing is for your project—and please note, there might be more than one type of "unit", since your application has multiple layers. For example, unit testing for a web project might encompass testing each class on the server and testing each JavaScript function. Feel free to have more than 3 levels of tests.

The Agile Test Automation Pyramid concept from Mike Cohn[1] states that you should have far more unit tests than integration tests, and more integration tests than end-to-end tests. This arrangement properly recognizes that there are many more small units and therefore more tests needed at this level. Note that this requires developers, who create the unit tests, to be primary contributors to the testing effort.

---

[1] http://www.mountaingoatsoftware.com/blog/the-forgotten-layer-of-the-test-automation-pyramid

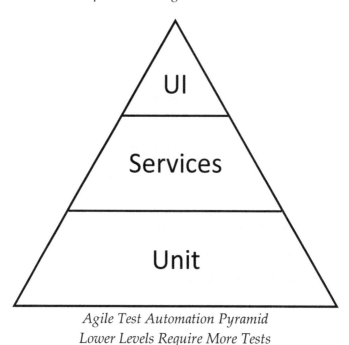

Agile Test Automation Pyramid
Lower Levels Require More Tests

Follow the Agile Test Automation Pyramid:
unit tests > integration tests > end-to-end tests

Mocking

When creating unit tests, there is sometimes a need to substitute a dependent object with a *mock object*—one that looks exactly the same on the outside, but simulates what the real object does. For example, the code you are testing might depend on an object that provides the current date; it would be convenient for testing purposes to use an object that can provide past or future dates. Or, you might want to replace an object that normally queries your database with an object that returns randomly-generated test data.

There are several reasons why you might want to use a mock object:

- The real object has not been developed yet.
- The real object is complex or slow and you need a fast, lightweight object for testing.

- The real object depends on real-world conditions that are inconvenient for testing, such as time of day or human activity.
- You need a version of the object that can generate its own test data.
- You need a version of the object that can generate its own events.

Mock objects can range from simple objects to elaborate simulations.

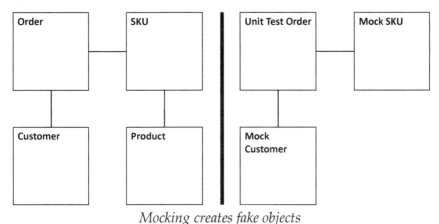

| Order | SKU | | Unit Test Order | Mock SKU |
| Customer | Product | | Mock Customer | |

Mocking creates fake objects

Mocking frameworks can be helpful in creating mock objects. For example, a mocking framework can take an interface and generate a complete class for it that returns default values—which you can then customize.

User Interface Testing

User Interface testing validates the user-facing parts of the software, via the application's access points such as a web site, desktop application, or mobile device. Testing the user interface should include exercising the screens and visual elements to ensure they deliver the intended user experience.

UI testing usually involves validating the implementation details match design comps and wireframes. It can also include usability testing and accessibility testing.

Usability Testing tests user responses to the user interface to gauge how usable the solution is. This is usually conducted by the

User Experience designers, and the results are used to refine the user experience design.

Accessibility Testing tests alternative methods for interacting with the software are working correctly, usually in support of disabled users. For example, a web site might be tested with keyboard only to ensure it can be used without mouse; or accessed with a screen reader.

As a developer, your focus should be on ensuring you have faithfully implemented the UI design you have been given: it should work properly, and hold up well to unexpected user interactions.

Although there are ways to automate UI testing, that is usually a concern best left for your QA group: UI testing tends to be part of end-to-end testing. When you the developer are testing code you have just written, you want to see and feel what the experience is like: is it smooth, does it look right, does it perform well, is it intuitive?

Security Testing

Security Testing tests the authentication (identity), authorization (roles and permissions), auditing, and data privacy aspects of the solution.

The STRIDE list defines categories of attacks to consider:

- **S**poofing identity: accessing and using another user's authentication information. For example, illegally accessing another user's credentials.
- **T**ampering: malicious modification of data. For example, making unauthorized changes to a database.
- **R**epudiation: a user can deny performing an action and there is no way to prove otherwise. For example, a user performs an illegal activity but insufficient information is tracked to determine who performed the action.
- **I**nformation Disclosure: making information available to users who are not authorized to have it. For example, employee pay stub information being visible to other employees.
- **D**enial of Service: denying service to valid users. For example, crashing a web server resulting in unavailability of the application.

☐ Elevation of Privilege: a user gaining privileged access. For example, a user who should be only able to view information becomes able to also update and delete information.

After your own team performs its security testing, *penetration testing* may be in order. In penetration testing, an outside security firm attempts to infiltrate your system using manual and automated attacks—but only for the purpose of revealing vulnerabilities, not exploiting them.

Performance Testing

Performance Testing measures the availability, responsiveness, processing speed, scalability, or stability of the solution under a variety of workloads. Performance tests are most credible when performed on production hardware. Testing often includes creating a *baseline* of test results; changes to the software can then be *benchmarked*, comparing test results against the baseline to see whether performance has improved or not. The best approach to baselines and benchmarks is to follow industry performance standards.

Load Testing tests that the system can continue to operate under a specific level of load, such as *n concurrent users*. For example, if you were targeting a peak load of 2,500 concurrent users, you would use load testing to verify the application's ability to support that target. In load testing, an Endurance Test or Soak Test determines whether the system can sustain that load over time.

Stress Testing tests reliability under heavy workloads. It can reveal bugs or points of failure that only appear under high load. In stress testing, a Spike Test causes a sudden short burst of increased load.

Compatibility Testing

Compatibility Testing tests how well the software works in a particular hardware/software configuration. A web solution might undergo compatibility testing with specific web browsers or mobile devices. Here are some examples of compatibility testing:

• Verifying your application works on multiple operating systems.

- Verifying your application's UI conventions don't look out of place (for example PC vs. Mac, or iOS vs. Android)
- Verifying your application works with supported database products.
- Verifying your application works with supported browsers and mobile devices.

In compatibility testing, it's important to set proper expectations about what areas should be identical vs. reasonably equivalent across environments. For example, in browser compatibility testing you should expect some elements to be rendered identically but not typography or form input controls.

Compliance Testing

Compliance Testing or Conformance Testing is an audit to determine whether the software meets a defined standard. For example:

- Compliance with an industry standard, such as the PCI standard for credit card processing.
- Compliance with a government standard, such as the Health Insurance Portability and Accountability Act (HIPAA).
- Compliance with an organization standard, such as a company's HR policies.

Compliance testing may involve:

- Confirming a data format.
- Confirming a process.
- Confirming an integration with an external service.
- Confirming a development or quality process.
- Confirming documentation meets a standard.
- Confirming sensitive information is protected.

The criteria for the standard governs the specifics of testing. A subject matter expert may be needed to help design tests or perform tests.

Monkey Testing

Monkey Testing uses automation to generate random interactions and data. The "monkey" is the program generating the input or interactions. For example, random text strings could be entered into text boxes on a form.

Why do it? Monkey testing introduces an element of chaos into testing, and can find flaws not found by structured testing because it's actions can't be anticipated. If your application will be exposed to the outside world or to a large internal audience, there's no telling what users might do.

Fuzz Testing is similar to Monkey Testing, but only involves random data—not random interactions.

User Acceptance Testing

User Acceptance Testing (UAT) tests the near-final solution with some of the intended users of the system. Stakeholders may also monitor or take part in the testing. Its purpose is to assess application readiness for its intended use. It is usually the last type of testing performed, and may be combined with usability testing.

UAT gauges how well users in target personas are able to perform real-world tasks with the software. For example, a time and billing system for consultants might have consultants, contractors, managers, and accounting personas participating.

When users have trouble performing tasks during UAT, this can reveal a need for documentation and training improvements; clarify or add to requirements information; or show that a technical design doesn't' work well in practice.

Making Your Code Testable

Every developer should invest in creating automated unit tests and integration tests. The alternative is a lot of manual testing, which really means you will not do enough testing. With a good collection of automated tests, you can not only test your current work but have an easy way to determine down the road whether some other change has impacted your functionality.

Design your code with testability in mind. You have the responsibility to unit test your work comprehensively, and if your code isn't easily testable you will be forced into mostly manual testing. If your QA group does automated testing, making your code highly-testable will benefit them as well.

Your objective, then, is to ensure your code does not hamper good test coverage. A great approach to this is to review the Conditions of Acceptance in your story and try to come up with a unit test or integration test for each of them (or as many as possible; let's acknowledge up front that some COAs may be difficult to unit test, such as "error messages should be user-friendly").

Once you have a set of tests in mind, you'll need to determine how well your code allows each test to be performed and make adjustments where a test can't be performed. Even better is to take a *test-first* approach, where you design the tests before you write your implementation.

Design your code with testability in mind.

What makes some code difficult to write unit tests for? Let's consider several categories.

Automation-unfriendly User Interfaces

When automated tests are created for web user interfaces, having Ids for all significant UI elements is extremely helpful. Otherwise, indirect methods have to be used such as CSS selectors which are more fragile. Assign Ids to input controls, buttons, links, clickable elements, and prominent text.

Using unique RESTful URLs is very helpful: it allows tests to know where they are with confidence. Single-page applications that show and hide UI elements are much more challenging to automate as it can be tough to discern what is going on in the UI.

Pages that are not predictable are also very difficult to write UI tests for. A pages might be unpredictable because it continues where a user left off, such as a wizard that returns to the last step; or because it persists UI state, such as a user-configurable dashboard. These are nice behaviors from a feature perspective, but are challenges to UI test writers. Consider providing a way for a test to get to a known starting point, such as an optional URL parameter that resets state to known conditions.

Poor Cohesion

Some code has poor cohesion (if the description of a class or function includes the word "and", that's a tip off). This kind of code can complicate testing because it forces you to take all of its functionality. For example, a class that both represents an invoice *and* generates an invoice report would be better separated into an invoice class and a report class.

Inability to Control Variables

A test should be able to control all variables it is entitled to. If the code to be tested uses internal values that the test can't override, that can obstruct good testing.

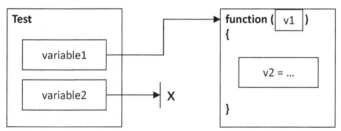

Code that doesn't allow a test to control a needed variable

The function below checks whether a customer payment is overdue by comparing its due date against today's date. The developer reasoned that the only parameter needed is the customer payment. Which is perfectly sensible if you aren't thinking about testability.

```
bool IsCustomerPaymentOverdue(CustomerPayment payment)
{
    ...
    today = DateTime.Today;
    ...
    if (today >= payment.DueDate) ...
}
```

If the function retrieves the current date itself, that will be fine in the real world but it causes a testing difficulty, because in our testing we would like to try different values for "today". In order to support testability, the developer could provide a way for the date to be passed in to the function as a parameter. Now you can easily write tests to exercise how the function behaves in past, present, and future scenarios.

```
bool IsCustomerPaymentOverdue(CustomerPayment payment, Date
today)
{
    ...
}
```

Dependencies

If the code to be tested has dependencies on other classes with implementations that are unwanted at test time, consider using the Dependency Injection (DI) pattern which passes interfaces as parameters. This approach permits test code to mock out unwanted implementations.

For example, imagine you want to test your C# Avatar class, which has a dependency on a CloudStorage class to store and retrieve user profile images from a cloud storage account.

```
public class Avatar()
{
    private CloudStorage storage;

    public Avatar()
    {
        storage = new CloudStorage();
    }

    public Url GetAvatar(String username) { ... }
    public void SetAvatar(String name, String filepath) { ...
}
    public Url GetManagerAvatar(String username) { ... }
}
```

The problem with this class is that when it is tested, it wants to use the same place for storage that it uses when run normally. When running tests, we might want to use a different place for storage and perhaps even a different type of storage, such as the local file system. The class in its present form does not allow us to override how it performs storage. To change that, we can abstract CloudStorage into an IStorage interface, and allow the storage object to be passed in to the class's constructor. By defaulting the IStorage parameter when a value isn't specified, we can preserve the original behavior and calling signature for the class so that there's no impact on existing code that uses it.

```
public interface IStorage
{
    public byte[] GetFile(String folder, String name);
    public void PutFile(String folder, String name, String
filename);
    public byte[] DeleteFile(String folder, String name);
}


public class Avatar()
{
    private IStorage storage;

    public Avatar(IStorage storage = null)
    {
        if (storage==null)
        {
            storage = new CloudStorage();
        }
        this.storage = storage;
    }

    public Url GetAvatar(String username) { ... }
    public void SetAvatar(String name, String filepath) { ...
}
    public Url GetManagerAvatar(String username) { ... }
}
```

Now we can test this class in isolation.

Testable Code Still Needs to be Clean Code

Making your code testable is important, but don't sacrifice the clean readability of your code in the process. For example, if you need to add many parameters to a function for the sake of enabling more tests, the resulting code may look more complex and less clear, including places where it is invoked by callers. You can combat this with function/constructor overloads, or parameter defaults, or passing structures instead of large numbers of parameters.

4 FUNCTIONAL TESTING

> *"Correctness is clearly the prime quality. If a system does not do what it is supposed to do, then everything else about it matters little."* –Bertrand Meyer

Narrative

Jon next wanted to spend some time with the programmer who knew the most about testing their own work; but when he inquired who that would be, he was given two names: Brian and Howie. He went to visit Brian first, only to find Howie was there too, working right alongside him. "Can one of you spare some time to discuss developer testing with me?" asked Jon. "You should talk to both of us," said Brian. "We work as a pair, and we help test each other's work."

"Great!" said Jon appreciatively. "I presume you're writing unit tests." said Jon. "Every place I've ever worked, the developers have been

expected to write unit tests." "We do write unit tests whenever we create or update a class," said Brian. "And integration tests whenever we create a server action or API." added Howie. "But we've just finished implementing a story, and we need to test that."

"Test it how?" asked Jon. "There are so many kinds of testing to choose from. There's unit testing, integration testing, system testing, black box testing, white box testing, UI testing... the list is endless. Which tests should a developer be doing when they finish a story?"

"That's easy—Functional Testing." said Brian. "You mean, you only do one kind of testing?" asked Jon, a bit surprised. Brian continued, "Functional testing has to come first. There's no point in doing any other kind of testing until you know your code works when used properly. Otherwise what you've done is wrong or incomplete." Howie added, "Once your functional tests pass, you're ready for other kinds of testing such as hostile testing."

"All right," said Jon as he took careful notes. "Let's discuss Functional Testing then." Howie immediately jumped to his feet, donned a headset, and announced in a loud voice, "My name is Arthur, how may I be of service?" Jon paused, not understanding. "What Howie means," interjected Brian, "is that we're testing the call center module today, and we have a persona for a call center rep named Arthur. Howie likes to do a little method acting when we're doing functional testing. He even dresses the part sometimes."

Jon said, "I thought personas were just for the UX group." "No, they're for everyone." corrected Brian. Each member of the team must understand our different users and what they need to accomplish." "'As a call center rep, I need to easily call up customer information during phone calls.'" said Howie, quoting the first part of a story. Brian added, "We have conditions of acceptance for what the software needs to do for a call center rep. As we test our module, we'll go through the same sequences a call center rep would, looking to confirm each condition of acceptance along the way."

Jon observed as the two set up initial conditions for their test and walked through a sequence they had scripted. After each user interaction, they checked that certain conditions were true. "Where did you get that script?" asked Jon. "We created it from the story and its conditions of acceptance." said Brian. "I imagine you also used your knowledge of the code to design the test." said Jon. "You couldn't be more wrong." said Howie. "In Functional Testing, we only use the requirements. We have to put aside what we know of the internals."

"And teaming up as a pair? How does that work?" asked Jon. "We programmers have blind spots when it comes to testing our own work." said Brian. "Having a second set of eyes helps find more of the issues."

Jon watched the pair complete their test sequence. Two issues were found, which were quickly addressed. In the second run of the test sequence, everything seemed to function as expected, so he asked "It looks like you're done here. That didn't take long." "We're far from finished." said Brian. "We need to test variations in the sequence to exercise different options the user can select. We need to test the call center rep and call center supervisor roles." "And," said Howie, "We need to test on several different browsers and devices."

"One last question," said Jon. "How do you know when you've done enough testing?" "At a minimum, we're expected to find all the obvious problems." said Howie. "If we didn't do that," added Brian, "All that would happen is that QA would rapidly find issues and run up a large bug list." Jon nodded thoughtfully: he'd been in exactly that place in his last project.

Testing the Positive Use Case

Functional testing is *positive* testing: it checks that the solution meets its requirements when used as intended. In this type of testing, users don't make data entry errors, always perform operations in the expected sequence, and do nothing to surprise or stress the software. It is also *black box testing,* which means your expectations are based solely on the requirements, not what you know of the implementation.

You should perform functional testing of your solution <u>first</u>, before performing any hostile testing. There's a very good reason for this: if your solution doesn't hold up to friendly use, your core implementation is questionable: you might have to go back to the drawing board to get it right. There's no point in harsh testing if the software crumbles in a friendly environment.

There's a second reason for doing functional testing: it can uncover issues not found by other methods. Hostile testing techniques are based on assumptions about specific types of errors that might exist in the software. In functional testing, you are focused on acting as a user to get an activity done and are not trying to force a specific kind of failure.

Designing Functional Tests

A functional test of a software feature or business task involves the following:

1. Understand the intended behavior.
2. Create a test plan, a sequence of steps you will take and conditions to check.
3. Set up your test.
4. Sign in with an appropriate user identity.
5. Perform a valid sequence of interactions and data entry in the software to exercise the feature, as described in its stories. This is the test sequence you came up with in Step 2.
6. Observe the behavior and output of the software, comparing the observed behavior to the expected behavior.
7. Confirm the end state of the solution is correct.

1. Understand the Intended Behavior

Understand the behavior that is expected of the feature, which should be documented in one or more stories. This means re-reading the requirements carefully. Every detail needs to be accounted for in your test.

Come up with a checklist of conditions that must be satisfied. If your requirements include a Conditions of Acceptance section, that's your checklist. If not, develop your own checklist from the story. Add to your checklist anything that is "always expected" even if not spelled out in the story (such as mobile support or internalization).

It's quite possible you will need more than one functional test for your feature. If what you're testing consists of multiple user activities, tests are needed for each activity. If the user can choose different options in the course of performing an activity, tests are needed to exercise each option. If the feature behaves differently for users in different roles, tests are needed for each role.

Determine how many tests are needed, and what the
conditions are that must be satisfied.

---

2. Create a Test Plan

Create a test plan in which a particular user role will attempt to perform a certain activity. This should include a list of steps to follow with things to check along the way. Know what the navigation and data entry will be and how you expect the application to respond.

Your test plan should include:

- ☐ The user role intended for the test.
- ☐ Any setup required before the test starts, such as a data reset.
- ☐ A list of steps to follow: navigation, interaction, and data to enter; and things to check after each step.
- ☐ Final conditions: anything that should be true at the end of your test that needs to be confirmed.

Your completed test plan should cover every condition in your checklist.

---

*Create a Test Plan that includes test setup, the se-
quence of steps to perform / conditions to check, and
end-state checks.*

---

3. Set Up Your Test

Set up your test. Know the starting point state of the solution. For
example, if you plan to test adding an order you might want to
know how many orders already exist and what the highest order
number is before you begin.

For some tests, you may need to reset the data in the system to
a known state, or perform initialization tasks such as clearing a
browser cache.

Before starting your test, know the starting state.

---

4. Sign In with an Appropriate User Identity

Sign in to the solution with a user identity that has appropriate
rights to use the feature to be tested. Be sure the user identity
meets any conditions necessary for the test, such as "is an Administrator" or "is a member of the Marketing Dept.".

---

*Sign in as a user with the correct rights / conditions
for what you are testing.*

---

5. Perform Your Test Sequence

Perform a valid sequence of interactions and data entry in the
software to exercise the feature, as described in its stories. This is
the test plan you came up with in Step 2.

Steps 5 and 6 need to be done together. As you go through the steps, be sure to observe and compare.

6. Observe and Compare

Observe the behavior and output of the software, comparing the observed behavior to the expected behavior. Be sure to check each Condition of Acceptance in the stories. When you see differences, capture all the detail you can.

7. Confirm the End State is Correct

Confirm the end state of the solution is correct. For example, if you've just submitted an order there should be a new order in the system with correct details. You might be able to confirm end state correctness from within the application. If not, you can "look under the hood" such as directly examining the database.

Testing Variations

Whether your test passes or fails, test more than once to see if the behavior is consistent. Running three times is a good rule of thumb.

One functional test isn't usually enough to sufficiently validate a feature: variations need to be exercised as well. That can include testing with more than one browser or device; a different order of interactions; and changes in the data entered. If you have been provided with some examples of real-world tasks, model your test design after that.

Ensure you have a sufficient number of tests. If the feature to be tested supports multiple scenarios, test each of them. Minimally, test all of the mainstream scenarios.

It's logical to derive tests from each other, but beware of the evils of copy-and-paste: if you copy one test to create another, you need to review every detail to make sure you end up with the correct set up steps for what you're testing.

Example: View Sales Activity

Randy is a developer working on a sales management web application for call centers. His project team uses the Scrum software methodology. Randy is implementing a View Sales Activity backlog item that was assigned to him this sprint, and is preparing for Functional Testing.

Story

Here is the story and wireframe Randy was given to implement:

> ### View Sales Activity
> As a salesperson or sales manager, I want to be able to view sales activity for myself and my direct reports so I can determine current and past performance.

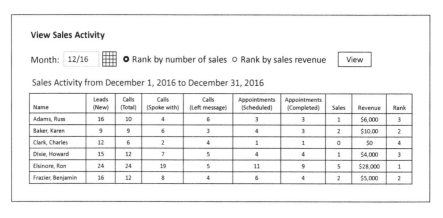

94

Conditions of acceptance:
- Accessed by selecting View Sales Activity from the Reports menu.
- Only available to users in the Sales department.
- Ability to select a month to report on. The default selection should be the current month.
- An option to rank by number of sales or sales revenue. The default should be *number of sales.*
- When the View button is clicked, a report of sales activity should be displayed. It should list a row for the current user and a row for each of their direct reports, in alphabetical name order. Each row should include salesperson name and counts of new leads, total calls, calls (spoke-with), calls (left-message), appointments scheduled, appointments completed, sales, and rank.
- When the *rank by number of sales* option is selected, the ranking is based on the number of sales made. #1 is highest sales, #2 is next highest sales, etc. More than one person can have the same rank if they have the same count of sales. When the *rank by sales revenue* option is selected, the ranking is based instead on total sales revenue.
- Needs to work on all supported browsers and devices.

Test Design

Randy understands the story well since he just implemented it, but re-reads it carefully to get a fresh perspective of what a user's experience should be and to remind himself of the Conditions of Acceptance.

Randy's first test plan is to test the story for a salesperson who has direct reports, sticking to default values:

<u>View Sales Activity - Test 1: Salesperson, defaults</u>
1. Sign in as user John Bird, a test user who is a salesperson and has several direct reports.
2. Navigate to Reports > View Sales Activity.

3. Confirm the default options are the current month and Rank by Number of Sales.
4. Click the View button.
5. Confirm a report is displayed with the expected columns.
6. Confirm there is a report row for John Bird and each of his direct reports.
7. Confirm the report counts match a database query Randy will run just before starting the test.
8. Confirm the ranking of salespeople by number of sales is correct.

The tests will need to be run multiple times, and performed on a number of browsers and devices since that is in the requirements. Randy doesn't have all of the devices he needs to support, but has a way to emulate them from his desktop.

Randy will need several derivative tests that have variations from his first test plan in order to cover the variables in the story:

- A test where the user specifies the month to report on.
- A test where the user chooses the Rank by Appointments Completed option.
- A test where the user has no direct reports.
- A test where the user is not in the sales department

View Sales Activity – Test 2: Salesperson, Month selection
1. Sign in as user John Bird, a test user who is a salesperson and has several direct reports.
2. Navigate to Reports > View Sales Activity.
3. Confirm the default options are the current month and Rank by Number of Sales.
4. Select a specific month.
5. Click the View button.
6. Confirm a report is displayed with the expected columns.
7. Confirm there is a report row for John Bird and each of his direct reports.
8. Confirm the report counts match a database query.

9. Confirm the ranking of salespeople by number of sales is correct.

View Sales Activity – Test 3: Salesperson, Rank by Revenue

1. Sign in as user John Bird, a test user who is a salesperson and has several direct reports.
2. Navigate to Reports > View Sales Activity.
3. Confirm the default options are the current month and Rank by Number of Sales.
4. Select the option to Rank by Sales Revenue.
5. Click the View button.
6. Confirm a report is displayed with the expected columns.
7. Confirm there is a report row for John Bird and each of his direct reports.
8. Confirm the report counts match a database query.
9. Confirm the ranking of salespeople by sales revenue is correct.

View Sales Activity – Test 4: Salesperson user, no direct reports

1. Sign in as user Kim Solo, a test user who is a salesperson with no direct reports.
2. Navigate to Reports > View Sales Activity.
3. Confirm the default options are the current month and Rank by Number of Sales.
4. Click the View button.
5. Confirm a report is displayed with the expected columns.
6. Confirm there is a report row for John Bird and each of his direct reports.
7. Confirm the report counts match a database query.
8. Confirm the ranking of salespeople by number of sales is correct.

View Sales Activity – Test 5: User is not in Sales dept.

1. Sign in as user Sam Outcast, a test user who is not a member of the Sales department.
2. Navigate to Reports. Confirm there is no View Sales Activity option.

As Randy performs his functional tests, he finds things are generally working well but finds a few issues to fix which he takes care of. In testing on various devices, he discovers his report doesn't fit on phone-size devices and renders poorly. He had overlooked that consideration originally, but his functional testing uncovered the omission. Randy discusses options with the project's visual designer, and they decide to use the same alternate layout for phones that worked well for another report.

Testing Your User Interface

The user interface is where technology and people meet. Test the UI at multiple levels: consider application/site, pages/screens, and individual controls. You are primarily looking to confirm that the user interface allows users to perform their objectives.

One of the things about testing a user interface that can be frustrating is when you're fuzzy on just what the intended experience is supposed to be. Software teams vary in how well they've formally designed their user experiences and communicated it to the developers. Even when that's done well, it's not unusual for user interfaces to regularly change over time as designs go through progressions. If you're not clear on what the intended experience is, find out. If no one can tell you, make some assumptions and document them. When you must make assumptions, you can appeal to consistency: how are similar tasks handled elsewhere in the application?

Not everyone uses software in the same way, and your testing should emulate several kinds of users. If your team maintains personas (user personality profiles), use them to think through how a particular type of user is likely to use the software.

Some users use a mouse the most, others touch, and others the keyboard. Can your application be used in all of the ways it is supposed to? You won't know unless you test them all. If your screens allow more than one way to do something, make sure each method is tested. For example, you might allow selection from a list through clicking but also support dragging: test them both. At times, you may have a feature where the total number of UI permutations cannot be fully tested without automation. In that case, test a reasonable variety and leave the exhaustive testing to QA.

Although there are ways to automate UI testing, that is a concern best left for your QA group. As a developer who is testing code you have just written, you want to see and feel what the experience is like: is it smooth, does it look right, does it perform well, is it intuitive?

In testing the user interface, check the following:

☐ UI matches the wireframes and visual design you were provided.

☐ UI conforms to general style guidelines for the application.

☐ Navigation, back-navigation, and breadcrumbs work as expected.

☐ Links are working and correct.

☐ Layout, borders, and spacing of elements is correct.

☐ Expected input validation is in place.

☐ Displayed information is formatted correctly.

☐ Each choice or option works correctly.

☐ Each element has correct position, width, height, and styling.

☐ Each element behaves correctly.

☐ Alternative input (such as ENTER or keyboard shortcuts) work.

☐ Error messages have correct content and style.

☐ Images are correct and have proper resolution and size.

☐ Mouse-over effects are correct.

☐ Displays and accepts input correctly across multiple languages. [If your solution has language support]

☐ UI is responsive and renders correctly on different size screens.

☐ UI is correct on each supported browser/device (use a device emulator if necessary).

☐ Spelling and grammar are correct.

Testing Provisioning

Depending on your application, provisioning may include installation/uninstallation, purchase, user registration, or sign-in/sign-out.

In testing provisioning, check all of the following that apply:
- ☐ Application can be installed.
- ☐ Application can be uninstalled.
- ☐ Application can be purchased or subscribed to.
- ☐ A new user can register with your application and use it.
- ☐ A returning user can sign in to the application and use it.
- ☐ Forgot password functionality works.
- ☐ Cancel account functionality, if present, works.
- ☐ User emails about provisioning actions are working and correct.

Testing Your Logic

Your application logic coordinates processing steps (including calculations, input/output, and decision making) into a flow of control. Use the requirements (not your code) to describe the expected logic, then use that to design your tests. you might find it useful to depict the logic in a flowchart, a decision table, or a UML activity diagram.

In testing application logic, check the following:
- ☐ Each path of possible logic flow is correct.
- ☐ Correct processing occurs in response to input or events.
- ☐ Business rules are being correctly applied.
- ☐ Computations are correct.
- ☐ Correct rounding is being applied.

Testing Data Storage and Retrieval

Functional test sequences frequently involve data entry and data retrieval, which need to be verified for correctness. A data-driven testing approach uses tables of inputs entered and outputs expected. If this can be combined with test automation, many variations of input can be verified with minimal effort.

In testing data storage and retrieval, check the following:

☐ Data queries retrieve correct data.

☐ Added, updated, or deleted data is stored correctly.

☐ Activity that should be audited is being logged correctly.

☐ Data is only accessible to authorized parties.

☐ Import operations function properly with valid input.

☐ Export operations produce correct output.

☐ Data built in to the software is correct, such as lists of locations.

☐ Sensitive data is encrypted or not stored as per requirements.

☐ Data lifetime requirements are correctly enforced.

☐ Database fields have correct data types.

☐ Database tables are indexed.

Testing Security

Much of security testing is naturally hostile. In your functional tests you can focus on confirming proper authentication, authorization and auditing behavior for users with valid credentials.

In testing security, check the following, for multiple users and roles:

☐ Sign in and sign out are operational.

☐ Credentials are required for access to secure areas.

☐ Users can access features appropriate to their role.

☐ Users can see information appropriate to their role.

☐ Users can perform actions appropriate for their role.

☐ Users can see information for other users appropriate for their role. For example, a manager might be able to see information about their direct reports.

☐ Sensitive information is encrypted or not retained in accordance with the requirements.

After Functional Testing

All of your functional tests should pass. If they don't, debug the issues until you are at a 100% pass rate. Be sure you have sufficient coverage in your tests, confirming each COA of your story and accounting for all variations.

Then, move on to hostile testing.

5 HOSTILE TESTING

> *"Be clear about the difference between your role as a programmer and as a tester. The tester in you must be suspicious, uncompromising, hostile, and compulsively obsessed with destroying, utterly destroying, the programmer's software."* – Boris Beizer

Narrative

Jon was curious what developers should do after completing Functional Testing. He visited Ross, an energetic young man with a reputation for thorough testing. He knew he was in for an interesting meeting when he noticed a plaque on the wall that read "D̶o̶n̶'̶t̶ Be Evil." Jon asked, "Can you tell me about hostile testing?" "I can do better than that —I'll show you." said Ross.

"Today I'm going to be testing a product ordering sequence —

hostilely," said Ross. "In fact, you can help. Why don't you sit down over here and begin an order for an X100 exercise machine." Jon complied, and soon had an order in progress. He noted the X100 he was ordering was the last one in inventory. "Okay, now what?" asked Jon. "Well, what kind of hostile tests can we perform?" asked Ross. Jon considered, and offered a number of unexpected interactions he could make on the order screen such as leaving out information; entering invalid data in some fields; trying to add the same product multiple times; and closing the browser window mid-order and later returning to the site. "Those are all good," said Ross, "but I've already tested everything I can think of in a single-user interaction. It's time to really challenge the software. We need to be evil.

"We're going to return to this exact starting point a number of times," said Ross, "Each time we'll complicate the order-in-progress with other interactions in parallel." Jon watched as Ross started another order for the same SKU, to confirm the software would not permit double-ordering of the same item. In the next test, an administrator attempted to delete the X100 product while an order was in progress. In another test the user's account was put on hold by an administrator mid-way through the ordering process. In yet another test the customer's shipping address was changed while an order was in progress.

"Come on," coaxed Ross, "Give me some ideas I haven't thought of." Jon thought furiously, then came up with "Let's return to the site to complete the order, but in two browser sessions at the same time," and "We could continue the order in one browser session and cancel it in another." "Excellent! You're learning!" Ross said with approval.

Jon left with a newfound-appreciation for ways to attack software. In a way he felt dirty, but he knew the application would be incredibly solid once it was able to stand up to all of these abuses.

Making Software Fail

Hostile testing is *negative* testing: you are attempting to make the software fail—and that is exceedingly difficult for most developers. It requires you to switch gears from being that programmer who looks upon his/her creation with love and affection, over to a tester who works their hardest to bring it down. It's kind of like tossing your children to the wolves: it goes against every instinct you have. Still, comprehensive testing starts with you and isn't a responsibility you can shirk without severely compromising quality. "Being evil" won't come naturally at first, but if you work at it you'll get better and better at finding vulnerabilities and exploiting them. Consider working with a buddy developer and helping test each other's work.

Do your utmost to make the software fail.

To make software fail, you need a means of attack. Here are some different kinds of attacks:

Equivalent Functionality Attacks

Some software offers more than one way to accomplish the same activity. For example, you might be able to bold text in a word processor or rich text control by toggling a toolbar button, or by pressing Control-B. Some applications have the same UI panel in more than once place. Usually the expectation is that the features will behave and look identically regardless of how they were summoned.

☐ Try accomplishing the same objective in different ways. Look for visible and functional differences.
☐ If the application offers express settings or a default configuration, compare that behavior to a custom configuration that should be equivalent.

Designing Equivalent Functionality Attacks

An equivalent functionality test has these parts:
1. Find a function in the application that has two or more ways of being accomplished.
2. Plan out the steps to perform each variation. Also plan whether you need to reset initial conditions so that each test variation does not affect the others.
3. Perform each variation and note the application's behavior and display for each.
4. Compare the variations and look for differences.

Example Equivalent Functionality Attack

Susan's marketing application has a mail merge feature that includes a template editor. A user creating or editing a template can insert mail merge fields by selecting them from a drop-down control, or by entering {fieldname} directly in the text. In both cases, the mail merge field is supposed to appear in the text in a highlighted style. Susan wants to test whether the two forms of selecting a field behave identically. She designs the following test:

Mail Merge Selection – Test 1: Select Fields from Drop-down
1. Sign in as user John Naher, a test user.
2. Create a new mail merge template.
3. Enter a paragraph of text in the editor.
4. Select First Name from the mail merge field drop-down.
5. Confirm the mail merge field appears in the text.
6. Repeat steps 4 and 5 for the other mail merge fields (Last Name, Company, Title, Address, Email, Phone).

Mail Merge Selection – Test 2: Select Fields in Text
1. Sign in as user John Naher, a test user.
2. Create a new mail merge template.
3. Enter a paragraph of text in the editor.
4. Enter {First Name} in the editor.
5. Confirm the mail merge field appears in the text.

6. Repeat steps 4 and 5 for the other mail merge fields (Last Name, Company, Title, Address, Email, Phone).

When Susan performs these two test variations, she notices a difference: although both tests insert the mail merge field at the current insertion point in the editor, test variation 1 does not move the insertion point past the field whereas test variation 2 does. The feature thus acts slightly differently—a bug which needs to be resolved.

Timing Attacks

Some software is guilty of making faulty assumptions about timing. For example, consider an order page that checks for available inventory when the page loads but never thereafter; if the user takes a long time to complete the form (or even if they don't), it's possible the item they want to order may no longer be available.

☐ Try starting a process and taking a long time to complete it; cause conditions to change between starting and completing the process.

☐ If the software has any scheduled processing, such as overnight email deliveries or end-of-month reports, try moving the server date forward to see whether that prevents the processing from taking place.

☐ Try a search or report with criteria so broad the data retrieval time may exceed a database command timeout or web request timeout.

☐ If the software has a trial expiration period, try circumventing it by setting the current date to be in the past.

Designing Timing Attacks

The steps in a timing test are dependent on the nature of the vulnerability you wish to target. Below are the steps for a timing attack where conditions change between starting an action and completing it.

1. Find a function in the application that checks an initial condition which needs to remain true when the user completes the function.

2. Sign in to the application as a user with rights to use the function.
3. Navigate to the function so that it checks its initial conditions, then pause.
4. Change the conditions, either through action in a parallel session or by waiting.
5. Complete the function begun in Step 3 and see whether the application detects and handles the change in conditions.

Example Timing Attack

Jon's business dashboard application includes a task manager for users. When a task is performed, it is removed from the list of pending tasks. Jon wants to test what happens when the same user is logged in on two different browser sessions and tries to complete the same task. He designs the following test.

Task Manager – Test 1: Same User, Two Browser Sessions

1. In a browser session, sign in as any user who has tasks.
2. In another browser session, sign in as the same user.
3. In browser session 1, navigate to the Task List.
4. In browser session 2, navigate to the Task List.
5. In browser session 1, open the first task but do not complete it.
6. In browser session 2, open the same task but do not complete it.
7. In browser session 1, complete the task.
8. In browser session 2, complete the task.
9. Confirm the application realizes the task session 2 is trying to complete has already been completed and disallows duplicate processing.

When Jon performs this test, he finds the application is happy to process the same task twice. He realizes the task's status needs to be re-checked to prevent duplicate processing.

Business Rule Attacks

In business rule attacks you attempt to find ways to violate business rules in the software. Business rules are sometimes expressed in language that is imprecise or that fails to cover all scenarios. A single business rule can be tested for correctness of conditions, logic, and formulas. When you have multiple business rules, the interactions between the rules can also be tested.

- Failure to engage: look for paths through the software where the business rule should be applied but isn't. For example, if a business rule is upheld properly for new orders, is the rule still applied if you later edit the order?
- Wrong logic path: Try and send the software down an incorrect logic path, by entering atypical and edge case values; default values or empty values; or unusual combinations of values.
- Rule conflict: check whether you can get two business rules that are in conflict with each other to apply at the same time.
- Missed scenario: check for scenarios the business rule fails to address.
- Try a variety of input values to see if the business rule handles them correctly, including minimum and maximum edge case values and illegal values.
- Invalid date sequences: try invalid date range sequences, such as end date before start date, or start and end date in the past.
- HR policy conflict: check whether the business rule violates any HR policies.
- Compliance conflict: check whether the business rule violates compliance with industry or government standards you are required to conform to.
- Contractual conflict: check whether the business rule violates any contractual relationships.
- Try to get the business rule to allow something it should not.
- Try to get the business rule to disallow something it should allow.
- Try to get the business rule to perform a divide by zero calculation.
- Use edge case values to get a calculated result to overflow or

underflow.
- ☐ Try edge case input values for dates to see if computed future dates such as due dates are valid.

Designing Business Rule Attacks

A business rule attack must be tailored to the rule being tested, but in general has these parts:
1. Have an area of the software in mind where a business rule is enforced.
2. Devise a test to exploit a suspected weakness in the rule. This may involve data entry of an invalid value, a combination of inputs, a combination of entered data and missing data, an unusual sequence, or a scenario the rule fails to consider.
3. Perform navigation and data entry in accordance with the test you have devised.
4. Look for evidence the business rule did or did not perform correctly, either from the user interface or underlying data.

To test multiple business rules that have intersection, it's important to have clarity about their interactions; else it's difficult to design proper tests or recognize defects. Create a decision table to represent how the business rules interact:
1. In the first column, list the business rules in a Conditions section.
2. Below that (still in the first column), list outcomes in an Actions/Outcomes section.
3. Create columns with Y/N or True/False values such that all combinations of conditions are accounted for.
4. Using the rules, determine which outcomes apply for each combination.

With a valid decision table in hand, you have everything you need to design tests and evaluate the correctness of results. A sample decision table appears below for the set of rules
A. The charge for a cup of coffee is $3.00.
B. Customers get 1 free cup of coffee on their birthday.

Conditions	1	2	3	4
Customer orders cup of coffee	N	N	Y	Y

Is customer's birthday	N	Y	N	Y
Actions/Outcomes				
Charge for cup of coffee	0	0	3.00	0.00

Example Business Rule Attack

Jim is working on a Paid Time Off application, which is required to honor the follow rules regarding vacation time:

A. *Employees get no vacation in their first year.*

B. *Employees earn two weeks of vacation per year worked, awarded on their anniversary date.*

C. *Employees who have been with the company for 5 years or more earn three weeks of vacation per year worked.*

D. *Unused vacation time > 4 weeks is forfeited on employee's anniversary date.*

Jim fashions the following decision table from the rules:

Conditions	1	2	3	4	5	6
New employee	Y	N	N	Y	N	N
Worked >= 1 yrs and < 5 yrs	N	Y	N	N	Y	N
Worked >= 5 yrs	N	N	Y	N	N	Y
Unused vac. time V <= 160 hrs	Y	Y	Y	N	N	N
Unused vac. time V > 160 hrs	N	N	N	Y	Y	Y
Actions/Outcomes						
Hours earned on anniversary date	0	80	120	N/A	80	120
Hours lost on anniversary date	0	0	0	N/A	V-160	V-160
Net change in vacation hours	0	80	120	N/A	80-(V-160)	120-(V-160)

With the decision table in hand, he designs the following test, designed to test boundary values in the unused vacation time rules.

<u>Order Points – Test 1: Vacation Time Accrued</u>

1. Sign in as a new employee.
2. Following the table below, perform the following for each row:

a. Advance the date by 1 year to next anniversary date.
b. Check employee start of year vacation balance against expected result in table.
c. Sign in as employee.
d. Request V hours of vacation time.
e. Sign in as manager.
f. Approve vacation request.
g. Check employee end of year vacation balance against expected result in table.

Years Worked	Hrs Awarded	Start Yr Balance	Vac. Hours Used	End Yr Balance
0	0	0	0	0
1	80	80	40	40
2	80	120	40	80
3	80	160	40	120
4	80	160	40	120
5	120	160	160	0
6	120	120	80	40
7	120	160	80	80
8	120	160	160	0

Form Control Attacks

In form control attacks you attempt to find vulnerabilities through interactions with controls (invalid data attacks are covered separately in the next section). Some inputs involve entry of text, such as names or comments. Some text input has data type limitations such as integers, currency amounts, and dates which place limitations on the acceptable characters and format. Other inputs involve selection from a set of choices, such as a drop-down select list, check boxes, radio buttons, range sliders, or a carousel control. Beyond the basic controls there are third-party controls that are more complex, such as calendar controls.

General

☐ Test that required fields are required and optional fields are optional.

□ Test correctness of position on form.

□ Test correctness of height, and width.

□ Test control is sufficiently sized for the data it needs to show or collect (in each supported language).

□ Test correctness of colors, fonts, and other styling.

□ Test that interaction with the control causes expected events to fire.

□ Test that fields are sized and placed acceptably on mobile devices.

□ Test that fields support alternatives to mouse interaction, such as keyboard or touch.

□ If web controls are expected to have Accessible Rich Internet Application (ARIA) attributes, test them using a screen reader.

□ Look for improper spelling or grammar.

□ Test whether cursor changes when hovering over an element that can be interacted with.

□ Test whether mouse hover or touch summons expected elements such as tooltips or pop-up dialogs.

Form

□ Enter fields in an unusual sequence; return back to earlier selections and change or clear them.

□ Test that related fields coordinate as expected. For example, if selecting a country is supposed to change the postal code field, verify that happens.

□ If there are input fields that interact with other input fields, try to find combinations that permit invalid values to be entered.

□ Test whether the form or site explains a privacy policy.

□ For web forms, open the F12 developer tools JavaScript console and check for error messages or console log statements. Try using the page with the console open; JavaScript *debugger* statements in the page will halt execution.

□ Test that the layout of controls is rational.

□ For software supporting localization, test whether left-to-right and right-to-left layout is correctly honored for locales.

□ Test the form's tab order, and look for controls that are not

tab stops but should be.
- ☐ Assess whether complex forms are difficult to use, or well-organized.
- ☐ Test whether controls of the same type have consistent styling and behavior.
- ☐ Test that zooming the browser larger or smaller renders web form controls acceptably.
- ☐ Does the form look acceptable on large and small size screens?
- ☐ Check for unintended scroll bars.

Labels

- ☐ Test proper wording, spelling, and styling of labels for input controls.
- ☐ Test longer values (such as a translated label in a language like German) can be fully displayed.
- ☐ Test wrapping of text is not rendered sloppily.
- ☐ Test label alignment is correct.
- ☐ Look for inconsistencies in punctuation or capitalization or terms.

Text Box

- ☐ Test default values are applied. When nothing has been explicitly entered, does the software use the expected default value?
- ☐ Try characters that should be filtered out, such as nulls and non-printable characters.
- ☐ Try entering fewer characters than the minimum length, or more characters than the maximum length.
- ☐ Try pasting in very long text; sometimes pasting or drag-and-drop can exceed the intended maximum length of an input box.
- ☐ Try entering unusual content, such as pasting in rich text, HTML, or XML.

Select Box

- ☐ Try not selecting a value.

☐ Try selecting the "make a selection" option.

☐ Try selecting multiple values.

Radio Buttons

☐ Try not selecting a value.

☐ Try selecting multiple values. Ensure one and only radio button in a group can be selected.

☐ Try selecting a button in one radio button group to see if buttons in other groups are affected.

☐ Test whether each radio button can be selected by keyboard.

☐ Try selecting each button by mouse and by keyboard.

Check Boxes

☐ Test whether any combination of check boxes can be selected.

Buttons

☐ Try clicking a button multiple times.

☐ Test the enabled/disabled state of buttons as you interact with the form.

☐ Test whether buttons in a group show state correctly.

Video and Audio Controls

☐ Test rapid clicking of play/pause/stop controls.

☐ Test navigation forward and backward.

☐ Test zoom to full screen and exit full screen.

Hyperlinks and Navigation Controls

☐ Click link to verify it transfers to a valid and correct location.

☐ Confirm breadcrumbs read correctly and work forward and backward.

Clickable Elements

☐ Confirm clicking element performs intended action.

☐ Try clicking element repeatedly.

Scrollbars

☐ Test whether scrollbar allows all of its content to be viewed.
☐ Test whether adding an item to a scrollable list scrolls the newly added item into view automatically.

Designing Form Control Attacks

A form control attack has these parts:
1. Have an input field in an area of the software in mind to attack.
2. With the field's data type and intended behavior in mind, devise a series of interactions to test the field.
3. Perform navigation to the area to be tested.
4. Enter the sequence of values and/or interactions.
5. Look for unexpected control behavior, or evidence the form or its controls have gotten into a state that should not be possible.

Example Form Control Attack

Howard's shipping page is supposed to allow the user to select a shipping company from a dropdown, and then to select a level of service from another dropdown. When a selection changes in the first selection, the options change in the second selection.

Howard wants to try selecting options in both dropdowns, then deselecting the first drop-down, to see if the second dropdown stays visible with options that no longer apply.

Shipping Page - Test 1: Select and Deselect
1. Sign in as user Howard Monroe.
2. Navigate to the shipping page.
3. In the Shipping Company dropdown, select the first shipping company.
4. Check that the Shipping Service dropdown is populated based on the shipping company selection.
5. In the Shipping Service dropdown, select an option.
6. In the Shipping Company dropdown, reset the selection back to "--select a company--".

7. Check that the second dropdown is no longer populated.

Invalid Data Attacks

Entering invalid data is one of the most productive forms of software testing. This is similar to positive use case testing, except that some of the data entry has atypical, invalid, unexpected, or missing values. This certainly happens quite often in the real world.

When you enter invalid data, you are expecting the software to disallow the value; it should not allow invalid values to be used or stored in any way. Depending on the implementation, web form validation may happen as you enter characters into an input field; or client-side validation may occur when you click a submit button; or validation may happen server-side; or even when data is passed from the server to a database or service.

In each case, your attacks should begin with the available interactions and data entry for the control. For any kind of input element, consider what the allowable values should be and whether the element is required or optional. Then devise invalid values you can try. If the control accepts the invalid data, then next attempt to subvert form validation by submitting the form. Finally, try input data values that might cause problems as the data travels to a web server and on to a database. In addition to the kinds of invalid data values that occur to you, the list below may give you some additional ideas.

General

☐ Test whether data that is limited to a range has correct minimums and maximums.
☐ Test whether data entered propagates correctly to waypoints and its ultimate destination.
☐ If the field is for a non-text data type such as integer, currency, or date, try entering characters that aren't legal for the data type; or enter characters in a sequence that isn't legal for the data type, such as 12..6- for a number.
☐ Try values that are not valid according to the requirements.
☐ Try entering international characters.

☐ Try entering characters that might confuse web communication to the server, such as ampersand, single quote, double quote, percent sign, or angle brackets.

☐ Try characters that may cause SQL queries to fail, such as an apostrophe. For example: O'Malley

☐ Try entering '; followed by a SQL statement to see if SQL injection is possible. For example: '; `DROP TABLE Order`

☐ Try characters not valid for the input field's data type.

☐ Try characters that are valid for the data type, but in an incorrect order or quantity or precision. For example, values like 1.5.3, 4-, or 2.43965474 for a currency field.

☐ Try values that are out of range. For example, a negative price or a date like 12/32/16.

☐ Try spaces before or after input values. Are they trimmed away or treated as part of the input?

Input Boxes

☐ Try empty values. What does leaving an input field empty do? Is an input field containing only some spaces treated as empty?

☐ Try default values. When nothing has been explicitly entered, does the software use the expected default value?

☐ Try long values. Entering very long values may exceed an internal limit, cause a memory buffer overrun, or be longer than a database field permits. Try pasting in the text of an entire work of Shakespeare.

☐ Hold down a key on the keyboard and let it repeat.

☐ Enter HTML markup that contains angle brackets (< >), ampersands (&), pound signs (#), single quotes ('), double quotes ("), etc.

☐ Try more than one space between words.

☐ If your input field has a spell checker, try misspelled words.

☐ See what uNUSUAL cASing on input values does.

☐ Enter characters that should be disallowed.

☐ Enter text containing profanity,

☐ Paste Rich Text containing fonts, colors, bold, italics, underscores, newlines.

☐ Try JavaScript injection attacks. Example:

```
<script>alert('user-entered code is executing!');</script>
```
☐ If a profanity filter is supposed to be active, confirm it filters out unwanted words and phrases.

Numeric Input Boxes

☐ Enter a different data type, such as an entering text when an amount was expected.
☐ Enter a very long sequence of digits.
☐ Exceed the logical range, such as entering a negative value in an Age field.
☐ Enter more than one decimal point or minus sign in a numeric input field.
☐ Enter a decimal point or comma in an integer numeric input field.
☐ Enter a negative value where only a positive value should be allowed.

Date Input

☐ Enter out of range values, such as a month < 1 or > 12 in a date field.
☐ Enter non-existent dates, such as February 29th in a non-leap year.
☐ Test February 28-31 are correctly accepted or not, and don't cause miscalculations.
☐ Enter years in the past or future where they should not be allowed.
☐ Enter the time along with the date.
☐ In date ranges, enter an end date that is earlier than the start date.
☐ In a numeric field, enter I instead of 1 or O instead of 0.
☐ Assess how well date entry and data display work when logged in as a user whose regional settings have a different date format from the default.

Designing Invalid Data Tests

An invalid data test has these parts:

1. Have a form in mind where you will target one or more fields of input on the form.
2. Sign in to the solution with a user identity who has the rights to use the feature area to be tested.
3. Navigate to the target page where you will be making your attack.
4. Attempt entry of the invalid value(s) and note how the software responds.
5. Compare the observed behavior to the expected behavior. Was the invalid value disallowed? If the software was supposed to display a specific error message, did it appear?
6. Verify that invalid data values have not been used or stored.

Forced Error Attack

In this type of attack you deliberately trigger an error that the software is expected to be able to handle, and confirm the software correctly reports the error and performs compensating behavior. This type of test is important because error handling code is rarely exercised.

Some platforms and tools provide *fault injection*, where errors can be forced into the code dynamically at compile time or runtime. For example, fault injection would permit you to force an out of memory exception at a certain point in the code. If fault injection is not available, you could achieve a similar result by inserting statements into the source code that cause an error; however this can be a dangerous practice as you might fail to remember to remove the added code.

An alternative approach to forced error attacks is to try to get each error message in the code to appear solely from how you use the software. Some categories of errors are straightforward to replicate with this approach while others are difficult, such as an out of memory error.

Error handling code sometimes introduces side effects, such as not cleaning up the display or not returning to a proper state for continuation. Your tests should do more than just checking that an error was caught and reported; you also need to verify the software can continue to be used.

Designing Forced Error Tests

A manual forced error test has these parts:

1. Have an area of the software in mind where you will target an error message that the program code should generate in response to a specific error condition.
2. Know what corrective actions to expect from the application
3. Sign in to the solution with a user identity who has the rights to use the feature area to be tested.
4. Take whatever steps are necessary to induce the error message, such as improper data entry to trigger a validation error.
5. Confirm the proper error message is displayed, and any other corrective behavior expected of the application.
6. Verify the software can continue to be used successfully.

A fault injection forced error test has these parts:

1. Have an area of the software in mind and an exception you will inject.
2. Know what error message and corrective actions to expect from the application.
3. Instrument the application for fault injection, and configure the desired fault to be injected in the target area of the code.
4. Sign in to the solution with a user identity who has the rights to use the feature area to be tested.
5. Take whatever steps are necessary to get to the area of code where the fault triggers.
6. Confirm the proper error message is displayed, and any other corrective behavior expected of the application.
7. Verify the software can continue to be used successfully.

Navigation Attacks

Navigation attacks are the opposite of friendly functional testing, where you read the requirements, think like a user, and try to use the software in the intended manner. Here you are doing things in a completely unexpected order.

- ☐ Attempt to perform operations out of order, in an unusual sequence.
- ☐ First use the software correctly and record the URLs that the browser goes to. Then, try going to those same URLs in a random order.
- ☐ In wizard interfaces, go back and forth among the steps. Are the screens correct, and is previously entered data retained?
- ☐ Try alternate ways to get to the same place in the software. Does the solution behave consistently?

Security Attacks

Security testing is hostile by nature, but in your testing you should be careful to be a *white hat* hacker, meaning you are looking to uncover vulnerabilities but not actually cause damage. As security testing may cause data loss or crash the application, take measures to ensure you can return back to a good starting point.

A successful security attack may open the door to additional attacks. For example, once you are able to falsely authenticate yourself you are then able to try data tampering attacks.

Spoofing Identity

Spoofing identity attacks attempt to gain and use another user's credentials.

- ☐ Try guessing a username. If you are to tell whether the username or the password field is incorrect from the application's Invalid Login message, that is a bug: the app has conveyed useful information to a hacker that will help them confirm when they have guessed a correct username.
- ☐ Try a dictionary attack, which is guessing a password by using a dictionary or word list of passwords to attempt. The application can guard against this by requiring strong pass-

words and by locking out an account after N invalid login attempts.
- ☐ Try to reverse-engineer a session cookie and change it. A non-encrypted or poorly-encrypted session cookie will be susceptible to modification.
- ☐ Try capturing a session cookie and re-creating it in another browser session.

Tampering with Data

Tampering with Data attacks attempt to maliciously change data.
- ☐ Try changing URL parameters. Once signed in to the system, note the format of URL paths and query parameters, both of which may contain data such as Ids. If you alter these values, are you able to modify data you should not be allowed to?
- ☐ Try modifying form input fields before a submit. Using the F12 developer tools built in to most browsers, can you use JavaScript or jQuery from the console to modify what a form will submit?
- ☐ Try capturing and replaying another user's web traffic to see if you can get the server to perform actions that are not authorized for the signed-in user.
- ☐ Try SQL injection attacks. In an input field that becomes part of a dynamic SQL statement on the server, follow a value with a semicolon and a dangerous SQL command. For example:

```
Smith';DROP TABLE Customer;--
```

Repudiation

Repudiation attacks take advantage of insufficient auditing and logging by an application, allowing a malicious user to deny their actions.
- ☐ Perform malicious actions such as deleting data, then "deny the act" and see if there is enough evidence logged to convict you.
- ☐ Try to subvert auditing, by getting it to log incorrect information or an incorrect user identity.

Information Disclosure

Information Disclosure attacks attempt to gain access to information that the signed in user should not be permitted to see.

- ☐ Try deliberately causing an error to see if the error message provides any information about system internals, such as database names or a stack trace.
- ☐ Try requesting or searching for unauthorized data.
- ☐ If the web site in turn communicates with other systems (such as a document management server or a report server), see if you are able to directly access those servers.
- ☐ Try hacking access to the database.

Denial of Service

Denial of Service attacks attempt to compromise the application's ability to serve its users.

- ☐ Try flooding the application with too many requests in order to slow it down or bring it down.
- ☐ Try crashing the application. Is there a single point of failure vulnerability such as a single server, or is there a farm of servers that provide redundancy to maintain application availability.
- ☐ Test whether there is application monitoring and alerts in place, such that a support person is alerted in the face of denial of service activity.

Elevation of Privilege

Elevation of Privilege attacks allow a user to gain access to privileges they are not entitled to.

- ☐ Try a session fixation attack, where you try to convince the application to re-use a session.
- ☐ When not signed in, try directly browsing to pages that should require the user to be signed in.
- ☐ Try directly browsing to a page that should only be accessible by an administrator or some other privileged role.

Designing Security Attacks

To test security comprehensively (and to design defenses), use threat modeling. Consider what the possible threats (vectors of attack) are and test each one. There should be countermeasures in place to prevent each type of attack.

To test security you need to think like a hacker and consider attacks that would be used to gain entry to a system and harm it. In addition, you should also think like an authorized user who becomes disgruntled; what kind of damage can an insider do, and how can that be limited and tracked?

Use the STRIDE list of security categories and design multiple attacks for each category (see Chapter 3).

Consider the threat model below which diagrams an authentication attack. One technique a hacker can use is to try guessing a username, hoping for confirmation in the invalid login error message that the username is correct. The mitigation is to have generic (non-specific) error messages that don't give away which part of the credentials are wrong.

With the username known, a hacker can try logging in repeatedly using a dictionary or word list of potential passwords. The mitigation is to require strong passwords, so that the password is never just a word. Secondly, locking the account after N attempts prevents many repeated attempts at authentication.

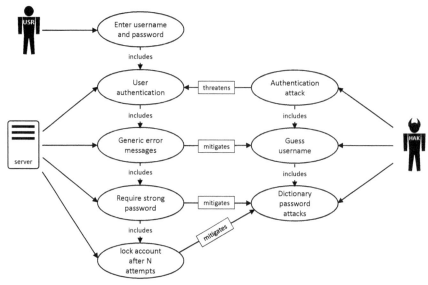

User Authentication Threat Model

The STRIDE list defines common attacks to consider:

☐ **S**poofing identity: accessing and using another user's authentication information. For example, illegally accessing another user's credentials.

☐ **T**ampering: malicious modification of data. For example, making unauthorized changes to a database.

☐ **R**epudiation: a user can deny performing an action and there is no way to prove otherwise. For example, a user performs an illegal activity but insufficient information is tracked to determine who performed the action.

☐ **I**nformation Disclosure: making information available to users who are not authorized to have it. For example, employee pay stub information being visible to other employees.

☐ **D**enial of Service: denying service to valid users. For example, crashing a web server resulting in unavailability of the application.

☐ **E**levation of Privilege: an unauthorized user gaining privileged access. For example, a user who should be only able to view information becomes able to also update and delete information.

6 AUTOMATED TESTING

"More than the act of testing, the act of designing tests is one of the best bug preventers known. The thinking that must be done to create a useful test can discover and eliminate bugs before they are coded—indeed, test-design thinking can discover and eliminate bugs at every stage in the creation of software, from conception to specification, to design, coding and the rest."—Boris Beizer

Narrative

Jon next met with Alice, a developer on the team who was also the build master. "How important is automated testing around here?" asked Jon. "Well, it's absolutely essential." said Alice. "I don't think we'd have a fraction of the confidence we do in our quality without it."

"What kind of automated tests does our team have?" asked Jon. *"Ideally, we want unit tests for all of our classes, integration tests for our services and APIs, and UI tests for end-to-end sequences."* said Alice. *"Which of those do you have the most of?"* asked Jon. *Turning to a nearby whiteboard, Alice sketched a triangle on the white board divided into 3 sections: UI at the top, Services in the middle, and Unit at the bottom. "This is our automation pyramid. The largest number of tests are unit tests because there are many small units of the software to test such as classes. The next largest group is the Services layer, which are integration tests of server actions, services, and APIs. The smallest number of tests are the UI tests, which cover end-to-end sequences. The percentage of tests we have out of the full set we'd like to have is what we call test coverage; right now our test coverage is about 80%."*

"And who writes all these tests?" asked Jon, afraid he knew the answer. *"Unit tests and integration tests are created by us, the developers."* said Alice. *"QA creates the UI automation tests. QA will sometimes take one of our integration tests or unit tests and extend them."* *"It seems like a lot of work,"* said Jon. *"It is a lot of work,"* admitted Alice, *"But it's far less work than manual testing, which has to be repeated over and over whenever there's a new build."*

Jon volunteered, "On my last project we were supposed to write unit tests, but we always ran out of time." Alice responded, "That's probably because you did them last. We've found we get more of our tests written if we use a test-first approach. That means we write the test before we write the implementation, instead of the other way around." Jon pondered what it would be like to write tests before the code to be tested even existed, a new concept for him.

Alice continued, "Of course, all of these tests wouldn't amount to much unless we run them whenever the software changes. That's the beauty of our Continuous Integration system: tests get run every time the software is modified." Jon perked up. "Actually, I've been meaning to ask you about that," he said. "One thing I don't like around here is how long it takes to make a check-in; I've waited as long as 20 minutes at times for a check-in, and if a check-in is rejected that gets multiplied two or three times over by the time I've corrected the issue and made the build system happy."

"And what," asked Alice pointedly, "would the result have been if the CI system didn't reject your check-in?" Jon thought for a moment, then admitted "There would have been breaking changes that affected the rest of the team. I begin to understand. The CI system is protecting us from each other."

"Let me tell you what things were like before we put CI in place," said Alice. "We have 10 developers working in 3 time zones. In any 24-hour period, there's the possibility of someone damaging the software because they made a mistake. For example, a UX developer would add a CSS file to the solution, but forget to add the new file to source control; or a back-end developer would change a class, unaware that the change impacted other parts of the solution. This broke things for the other team members and was highly disruptive.

"Once we realized how precarious a situation we were in, we decided to invest in Continuous Integration; and we all wish we had done it sooner. Now—as you've discovered—a breaking change is not permitted to pollute the solution. It's a safeguard that protects us from each other. Once a feature is complete and working, we make sure we have good coverage in our check-in tests. With that safety net in place, it's impossible to check in a change that breaks a feature. As long we keep this up our team moves forward, not backward."

Automated Testing

For you as well as your QA group, testing is hard work. Software can have a very large surface area, and testing it all can take a lot of effort—especially since software updates mean re-resting. Anything you can do to automate aspects of that testing will reduce manual labor. Creating a well-designed automated test is also work, but once created you can run it as often as you like, so the benefit is ongoing.

Testing Frameworks

To perform automated testing, you need a testing tool or framework for each tier of the solution that is to be tested. If you aren't already equipped with a means of doing automated testing, investigate putting one in place. Testing tools and frameworks vary in cost and capability and some are very expensive; but there are also a number of good testing frameworks that are free, such as Jasmine and QUnit for JavaScript testing.

Put automated testing in place for each tier of your solution if feasible.

Testing frameworks vary, but we can generally group them into two broad categories: User Interface Testing and API Testing.

User Interface Testing

UI Testing is tricky: testing tools have to simulate human interaction by issuing clicks, gestures, and keyboard input; wait for completion of processing; and "look" at what is displayed or rendered in response. Some UI testing tools provide record and playback abilities, simplifying the task of defining the interactions to perform. When elements of the UI are changed by the developers, UI tests may need to be completely re-created.

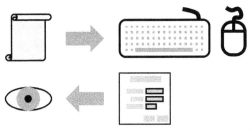

UI Testing Frameworks simulate interaction and check responses

UI Testing Example: Testing a Web Site with Selenium

Let's consider a UI testing example for a web site. Imagine you have an HR web site and would like to create a UI test for one of its pages, a Pending PTO Report. To get to the report, a user must first sign in, then navigate to the report. The pages look like this:

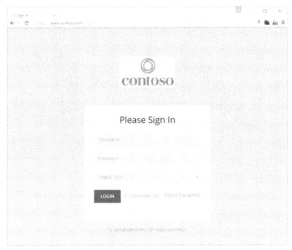

Contoso Login Page

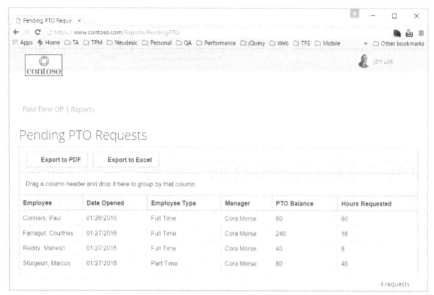

Contoso Pending PTO Requests Report

We can automate a test for this web sequence using Selenium WebDriver, a popular open source web UI testing tool. Selenium can be used with multiple browsers and integrates with a number of development environments. In our example, we'll drive the Chrome browser and integrate our tests with Microsoft Test Explorer in Visual Studio.

As a simple first-level test, we'll verify that we navigate to the report and expect the report to show the correct number of pending PTO requests. The sequence we need to automate is:

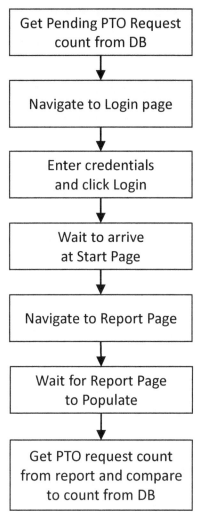

Pending PTO Request Report Test Sequence

1. Query the database to determine the number of pending PTO requests we expect to see on the report.
2. Next, using Selenium WebDriver, navigate to the login page, enter credentials, and login.
3. Wait for successful processing of the login and arrival at the application start page.
4. Navigate to the Pending PTO Request report page.
5. Wait for the report page to populate.
6. Determine the number of items listed in the report, and

compare it to the count from Step 1. Fail if the counts don't match.

The test will need to know the URLs of the login page and reports page, as well as the name of web elements that need to be interacted with. With those details determined, the following test can be written in C# for Microsoft Test Explorer:

```csharp
using System;
using System.Data;
using System.Data.SqlClient;
using Microsoft.VisualStudio.TestTools.UnitTesting;
using OpenQA.Selenium;
using OpenQA.Selenium.Chrome;
using OpenQA.Selenium.Support.UI;

namespace TestHR.UI
{
    // Test Pending PTO Requests Report.

    [TestClass]
    public class Test_UI_SampleReport
    {
        #region Variables

        private const String SITE_BASE =
"https://www.contoso.com";
        private const String USERNAME = "jonlee";
        private const String PASSWORD = "password...";
        private const String DATABASE = "Server=...";
        private IWebDriver wdriver = null;

        #endregion

        #region Initialize

        // Initialize the Selenium web driver.

        [TestInitialize]
        public void TestInit()
        {
            Console.WriteLine("Initializing Selenium webdriver");
            wdriver = new ChromeDriver(@"dependencies");
        }

        #endregion
```

```csharp
#region Tests

#region Test_PendingPTOReport

// Test Pending PTO Requests report

[TestMethod]
[TestCategory("UI")]
[TestCategory("Test_UI_PendingPTOReport")]
public void Test_PendingPTOReport()
{
    Console.WriteLine("Starting test: Pending PTO report");

    // Get pending PTO count from database

    int requests = 0;
    using (SqlConnection conn = new SqlConnection(DATABASE))
    {
        conn.Open();

        String query = "SELECT COUNT(*) FROM PTORequest WHERE Status='Pending'";

        using (SqlCommand cmd = new SqlCommand(query, conn))
        {
            cmd.CommandType = CommandType.Text;
            using (SqlDataReader reader = cmd.ExecuteReader())
            {
                if (reader.Read())
                {
                    requests = Convert.ToInt32(reader[0]);
                }
            }
        }

        conn.Close();
    }

    Console.WriteLine("• pending PTO request count in database: " + requests);

    // Navigate to the login page.
```

```
Console.WriteLine("• navigating to Login page");

wdriver.Navigate().GoToUrl(SITE_BASE + "/Login");
wdriver.Manage().Window.Maximize();

// Enter credentials

Console.WriteLine("• entering credentials");

IWebElement inputUsername = wdriv-
er.FindElement(By.Id("username"));
inputUsername.SendKeys(USERNAME);

IWebElement inputPassword = wdriv-
er.FindElement(By.Id("password"));
inputPassword.SendKeys(PASSWORD);

// Submit login

IWebElement goButton = wdriv-
er.FindElement(By.CssSelector(".btn"));
goButton.Click();

Console.WriteLine("• submitted login");

// Wait up till 30 seconds to see an element that
confirms we are on the start page

IWebElement breadcrumb = wdriv-
er.FindElement(By.CssSelector("#nav-main"), 30);

// Confirm we end up at the start page.

Assert.AreEqual(SITE_BASE + "/Menu", wdriver.Url);

Console.WriteLine("✓ at start page");

// Navigate to the Pending PTO Request report page

Console.WriteLine("• navigating to Pending PTO
Report");

wdriver.Navigate().GoToUrl(SITE_BASE +
"/Report/PendingPTO");

// Wait up till 30 seconds to see the report
```

```csharp
            IWebElement h2 = wdriv-
er.FindElement(By.CssSelector("h2"), 30);
            Assert.AreEqual("Pending PTO Requests", h2.Text);

            Console.WriteLine("✓ at Pending PTO Requests
page");

            // Get report item count

            Console.WriteLine("• looking for item count");

            IWebElement items = wdriv-
er.FindElement(By.CssSelector("span.k-pager-info"));

            Assert.IsNotNull(items, "item count footer label
not found");

            int requestCount = 0;
            if (items.Text.EndsWith(" requests"))
            {
                requestCount = Con-
vert.ToInt32(items.Text.Substring(items.Text.Length-9));
            }

            Console.WriteLine("✓ report request count: " +
requestCount.ToString());

            Assert.AreEqual(requestCount, requests, "Report
request count does not match request count from database");

            Console.WriteLine("✓ item count is correct");

            Console.WriteLine("End of Test");
        }

        #endregion

        #endregion

        #region Cleanup

        // Shut down the Selenium web driver.

        [TestCleanup]
        public void TestCleanup()
        {
            if (wdriver != null)
```

```
            {
                Console.WriteLine("Terminating Selenium web-
driver");

                wdriver.Quit();
                wdriver.Dispose();
                wdriver = null;
            }
        }

        #endregion
    }
}
```

When the test is run, Selenium WebDriver will launch Chrome and execute the test sequence, which you can watch on your desktop. When the test completes, a failure result looks like this:

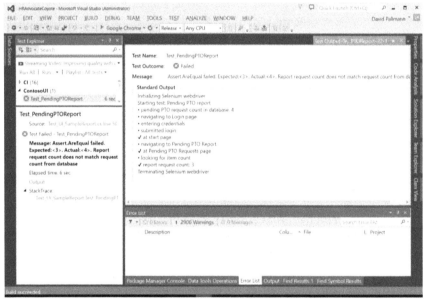

Failing WebDriver UI Test in Visual Studio

When the report and test are both correct, a successful result looks like this:

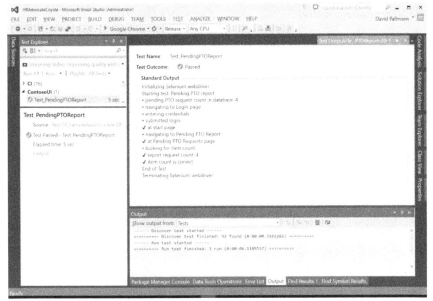

Passing WebDriver UI Test in Visual Studio

API Testing

API testing is comparatively simpler, bypassing the UI and invoking services, APIs, classes, or functions with test parameters and evaluating results to determine whether the expected functionality was carried out. An API result might be as simple as a true/false result, but could also be a complex object that needs verification.

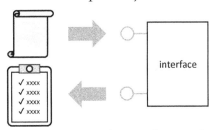

API Testing Frameworks invoke interfaces and verify results

In web solutions, API testing can often be applied for client-side JavaScript as well as for server-side APIs.

API Testing Example: Testing JavaScript with Jasmine

Let's consider an API testing example for JavaScript code. Imagine you have the JavaScript purchaseOrder object listed below and would like to create unit tests for it.

```javascript
// purchaseOrder object
var purchaseOrder = {
    submit: function () {
        ...
        return true;
    },
    lookup: function (poNum) {
        try {
            ...
            return true;
        }
        catch(e) {
            ...
            return false;
        }
    },
    total: function () {
        var total = 0.00;
        for (var i = 0; i < this.items.length; i++) {
            total = total + this.items[i].price;
        }
        return total;
    },
    orderNumber: 1005,
    items: [{
            name: "PRD001", price: 10.00
        }, {
            name: "PRD002", price: 5.00
        }, {
            name: "PRD006", price: 7.00
        }, {
            name: "PRD024", price: 2.00
```

```
    }]
};
```

JavaScript purchase order object to be tested

For our testing we'll use Jasmine, a popular open source test framework for JavaScript. Below are unit tests for this object, which will execute in script on a web page that also contains the purchaseOrder object. These tests inspect properties of the object and call its functions, asserting conditions that should be true if the object is working as intended.

```
// Jasmine tests for purchaseOrder object

// Test that purchase order object has expected number of
properties.

describe("purchaseOrder object", function () {
    it("has 5 properties", function () {
        expect(Object.keys(purchaseOrder).length).toBe(5);
    });
});

// Test that purchase order object has one or more line items

describe("purchaseOrder object", function () {
    it("has one or more line items", function () {
        ex-
pect(purchaseOrder.items.length).toBeGreaterThan(0);
    });
});

// Test that purchase order submit function returns true

describe("purchaseOrder object", function () {
    it("submit() returns true", function () {
        expect(purchaseOrder.submit()).toBe(true);
    });
});
```

```
// Test that purchase order lookup function returns true for
an existing P.O.

describe("purchaseOrder object", function () {
    it("lookup(<existing-po>) returns true", function () {
        expect(purchaseOrder.lookup('1005')).toBe(true);
    });
});

// Test that purchase order lookup function returns false for
an non-existent P.O.

describe("purchaseOrder object", function () {
    it("lookup(<non-existant-po>) returns false", function ()
{
        expect(purchaseOrder.lookup('7')).toBe(false);
    });
});

// Test that total function returns correct amount.

describe("purchaseOrder object", function () {
    it("total returns correct amount", function () {
        expect(purchaseOrder.total()).toBe(24.00);
    });
});
```

When the above test is run, successful output with all tests passing looks as follows, with all test results displayed in green.

Jasmine test run with all tests passing

When there is a failure, failing test results are shown in red and marked with an ×. You can drill into failing tests to see details on each failure.

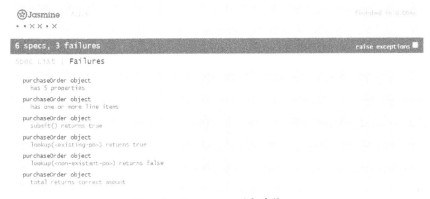

Jasmine test run with failures

Jasmine test failure detail

It's possible to integrate Jasmine with a number of development tools. Below is how the same tests look when Jasmine has been integrated with Microsoft Visual Studio. Integration like this allows the developer to test both their JavaScript code and server code from the same environment.

```
Test Explorer                                    ▾  ⌸  ✕
  ⚲  ▐▒ ▾  Search                                    ρ ▾

  ▶ Streaming Video: Improving quality with unit tests        ▾
  Run All │ Run... ▾ │ Playlist : All Tests ▾
  ⊿ Module [purchaseOrder object] (6)
     ⊘ purchaseOrder object has 5 properties            3 ms
     ⊘ purchaseOrder object has one or more line items   1 ms
     ⊘ purchaseOrder object lookup(<existing-po>) returns...
     ⊘ purchaseOrder object lookup(<non-existant-...     1 ms
     ⊘ purchaseOrder object submit() returns true
     ⊘ purchaseOrder object total returns correct amount
```

Jasmine integrated with Visual Studio

Continuous Integration

Breaking changes are a significant problem for development teams. Having previously-working code disrupted when multiple developers integrate their changes is both discouraging and counter-productive. Breaking changes often occur at a critical time: with a looming deadline, everyone is working at a frantic pace. Fortunately, there is an answer: Continuous Integration (CI).

Continuous Integration prevents breaking changes by combining test automation with source control check-ins. The general flow of a CI system is shown below. When a developer checks in code, the solution must build successfully on a build server and also pass a suite of tests as part of the check-in process. If the build fails or any of the tests fail, the check-in is rejected and code changes are not applied. CI thus protects the source code against breaking changes, and protects developers from each other. In a CI environment, developers can be safely checking in several times a day.

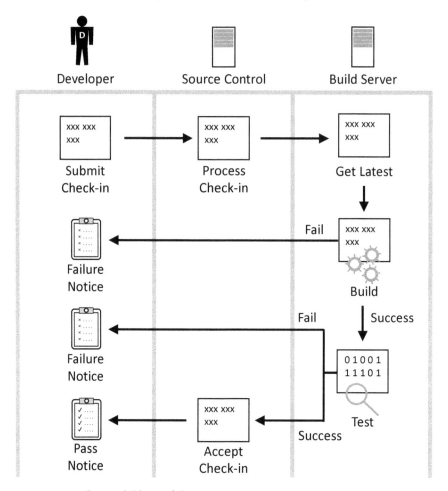

General Flow of Continuous Integration Systems

The effectiveness of CI is directly related to how comprehensive the check-in tests are. If only a few of your features have tests, or the tests are shallow, the value of CI is marginalized. If you have good test coverage, you can be confident that the code in source control has not taken a turn for the worse because all check-in tests have to pass in order for code changes to be accepted.

CI comes at a cost: check-ins take longer, and it can be frustrating to a developer when a check-in is rejected. For example, if a check-in takes 20 minutes and a developer's check-in isn't accepted until the third attempt, an hour has gone by. However, this isn't wasted time: it would have been far more disruptive if a breaking change entered source control and affected other developers on the team. The inconveniences of CI are well-worth the protection it provides. Other costs of CI include the initial configuring of the CI system, and the ongoing need to write check-in tests. Since developers should be writing unit tests all along, they can also be used as check-in tests.

Use Continuous Integration to protect source control
and other developers from breaking changes.

CI Example: Team Foundation Server

To illustrate CI in action, let's examine an implementation on the Microsoft platform where developers use the Visual Studio development environment and Team Foundation Server (TFS) for source control. TFS can perform builds on a build server on-demand, on a scheduled basis, and/or upon a check-in.

Peter is one of 10 developers working on the CommerceBoost team. He has just made some bug fixes, and is now going to check in his code changes. Upon submitting his check-in, he is reminded that it is only provisional, pending verification. Peter is now free to do other work while the build and check-in tests are processing. A notification will follow announcing pass or fail.

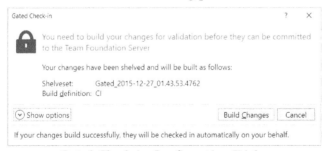

Gated Check-in Confirmation Dialog

Peter's initial check-in begins processing on the build server, and after about 10 minutes he receives a notification email explaining that the check-in was rejected because the build failed.

CommerceBoost-CI_20151222.7 - Check-in Rejected

Open Build Report in Visual Studio | Open Build Report in Web Access

Gated Check-in Build of CommerceBoost-CI (CommerceBoost)
Ran for 9.5 minutes (CPBuild01 - Controller), completed at Tue 12/22/2015 12:42 PM

Request Summary
   Request 1774   Peter Salamone   Check-in Rejected

Summary
  Debug | Any CPU
    1 error(s), 5384 warning(s)
    $/CommerceBoost/src/main/Solution/CommerceBoostWeb.sln - 1 error(s), 5384 warning(s)
       OrderUpdater.cs (59): 'CommerceBoost.Areas.Main.Models.Ordering.OrderViewModel' does not contain a definition
       for 'automaticPostingDate' and no extension method 'automaticPostingDate' accepting a first argument of type
       'CommerceBoost.Areas.Main.Models.Ordering.OrderViewModel' could be found (are you missing a using directive
       or an assembly reference?)
  Other Errors
    1 error(s)
       Exception Message: MSBuild error 1 has ended this build. You can find more specific information about the cause of
       this error in above messages. (type BuildProcessTerminateException) Exception Stack Trace: at
       System.Activities.Statements.Throw.Execute(CodeActivityContext context) at
       System.Activities.CodeActivity.InternalExecute(ActivityInstance instance, ActivityExecutor executor,
       BookmarkManager bookmarkManager) at
       System.Activities.Runtime.ActivityExecutor.ExecuteActivityWorkItem.ExecuteBody(ActivityExecutor executor,
       BookmarkManager bookmarkManager, Location resultLocation)

TFS Check-in Rejected Notice

After reviewing the notification, Peter realizes he failed to add a file to source control that is now needed by the build. He submits another check-in, and after some more waiting, Peter *again* receives a rejection message. This time the build has been successful, but one of the check-in tests has failed. Peter now realizes his code changes unintentionally impacted some other areas of the software. After making a correction and testing it locally, he once again submits his latest code changes. Again some waiting, and Peter is relieved to see that this time his check-is has been accepted.

CommerceBoost-CI_20151225.1 - Check-in Committed

Open Build Report in Visual Studio | Open Build Report in Web Access

Gated Check-in Build of CommerceBoost-CI (CommerceBoost)
Ran for 11.7 minutes (CPBuild01 - Controller), completed at Fri 12/25/2015 05:44 PM

Request Summary

Request 1776   Peter Salamone   Check-in Committed

Summary

Debug | Any CPU

0 error(s), 6 warning(s)

$/CommerceBoost/src/main/Solution/CommerceBoostWeb.sln – 0 error(s), 6 warning(s)

Associated Changesets

Peter Salamone. Bug 1681 fixed - Changeset 1518

TFS Check-in Committed Notice

7 ANALYZING & DEBUGGING

"Testing leads to failure, and failure leads to under-standing"—Burt Rutan

---

Narrative

Jon returned to his work area, his mind full of new concepts he was eager to put into practice. Right now, though, he needed to fix some bugs. He returned his attention to a problem that had been frustrating him since yesterday. Just then, lead developer Jeff dropped by. "How's it going? Anything I can help with?" asked Jeff. "Actually," said Jon, "Maybe you can give me some advice. I'm not making any headway on this problem in my JavaScript code. Sometimes it works and sometimes it doesn't."

"The best thing to do with a problem like that," said Jeff, "Is explain it to somebody else. Why don't you walk me through the code and explain what isn't working?" Jon wasn't sure that would help, but was willing

to try. "Well, it's silly really—the code isn't all that long. Here's my function to compute the total tax for an order. There's a loop that cycles through each item in the shopping cart, and inside the loop we perform an Ajax call to look up the tax for each item. By the time the total tax is displayed on the page, sometimes it's right but often it isn't."

Jeff took a moment to study the code, then asked "I see you're storing the tax that is returned." "That's right," said Jon. "The success function for the Ajax call stores the tax in the array element for the current item—oh wait, I see what's wrong now. The loop variable has surely changed by then, so I can't use it to index the item array. I don't know why I didn't see it earlier."

"Explaining problems to others really helps you see things." said Jeff. "What can you do to fix this?" "Well," said Jon, "I think I can just move this Ajax code into a function and pass the loop variable to the function. That should keep the value unchanged while the function executes." "I agree," said Jeff. "That's just what I'd do."

Bug Investigation

In order to fix a problem it needs to be understood. Some bugs are innately understandable, such as *Error message is displayed in the wrong color* or *Company name is misspelled*. Most bugs are less clear and require investigation, which is where analysis comes into play.

To analyze a bug, you need to frequently combine four areas: reproducing the bug; formulating and testing a hypothesis; studying the source code and using a debugger; and logging.

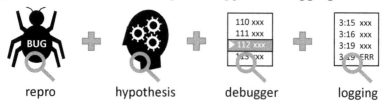

repro   hypothesis   debugger   logging

Bug investigation frequently combines these activities

Qualify Bugs Before Taking Action

Don't take it for granted that a bug report always describes an actual problem in the software. Failure to confirm a bug's validity can lead to wasted effort or making changes that are unnecessary or unwanted.

A bug report might really turn out to be:
- a suggestion
- a misunderstanding of the requirements
- an assumption that the requirements do not address
- intended behavior
- an unrealistic scenario
- an old problem that is no longer present
- premature testing of an area not yet released for testing
- an invalid test
- a duplicate of another bug
- insufficient/vague information that cannot be acted on
- a problem the development team is powerless to act on
- a problem better handled by someone else on the team
- a question
- incomprehensible

Take the appropriate action to reject or redirect these kinds of "bugs."

Filter out non-bugs. Confirm a bug is valid before acting on it.

Root Cause Analysis

During your analysis, strive to find the *root cause* of a problem. A root cause is the underlying real issue, not to be confused with secondary issues, effects, or symptoms. Root causes are specific, not general.

Finding the root cause may require you to dig deeper beyond your initial findings. Ask *why* as many times as needed to uncover the fundamental problem. For example, if a line of code is throwing an exception, ask why the exception is being thrown. If the exception is being thrown because a function returned an unexpected value, ask why the function returns an unexpected value. If the function is returning an unexpected value because a database record contains an unexpected value, ask how that happened; and so on. Note that some bugs have more than one root cause.

Dig to find the root cause of an issue. Treat the real problem, not the symptom.

Reproducing an Issue

The most common first step in analyzing a software problem is to reproduce it: if you can reproduce the problem, you can study the problem. When a problem can be reliably reproduced, narrowing in on the failing area of code is usually straightforward.

Reliable reproduction requires knowing the conditions for failure, which may or may not be fully understood at the start of an investigation. When you can't reproduce a bug as described, it's a good idea to connect with the person who originated the bug report and ask to see the problem. You may notice additional conditions for failure while observing the repro which can be added to the bug detail.

Once you are able to reproduce the problem, focus on finding the simplest circumstance in which the failure occurs. Remove unnecessary steps from the test case.

Reproducing an issue should be combined with looking at the code and forming one or more hypotheses that explain the failure. Changing the repro steps helps you prove or disprove your hypothesis. If your hypothesis is discredited, form a new one based on what you now know. Pay attention to test cases that fail as well as test cases that do not fail, using all the data available to you. If you don't have enough data, try more test case variations until a pattern emerges.

Find the simplest test case that exhibits the problem. Form a hypothesis about the cause of failure and refine it by varying the repro steps.

There are times when bug reproduction can be costly in terms of effort, time, or expense. Some bugs require significant set up and interaction to get to the failure point. Some bugs only fail after lengthy amounts of waiting. Some bugs incur a financial expense during their processing. When bugs have effects not worth incurring, look for ways to reduce the expense.

Bugs that Defy Analysis

Sometimes reproduction is evasive, as with some of the bug types discussed below. Not all bugs can be analyzed in the same way, and some resist analysis altogether. The categories below, while sometimes used humorously, are useful in recognizing the kind of bug you're dealing with and how best to analyze it.

Types of Bugs Requiring Different Kinds of Analysis

Bohrbug

A Bohrbug is a repeatable bug, one you can reliably reproduce and study. It is named after the Bohr model of the atom, which is very solid. This is the easiest type of bug to resolve by far.

By definition, this kind of bug is regularly reproducible which means the conditions for failure are known. You should be able to readily determine where the failing code is using standard debugging techniques and tools.

Heisenbug

A Heisenbug is a bug that defies analysis: attempts to observe the problem cause it to vanish or change behavior. It is named after Walter Heisenberg who discovered the *observer effect*, which states that observing a system inevitably alters its state.

For example, imagine you're trying to analyze a web page problem where an element that should be visible is not. You bring up the browser's F12 developer tools in order to study the issue but suddenly the element is now visible.

Another example is a server-side problem that never fails when single stepping through code in a debugger. This may indicate a race condition, where the timing differences of using the debugger avoid the problem.

Possible causes of Heisenbugs include failure to initialize variables; unexpected changes in the environment; and race conditions where there is a lack of proper synchronization. You may find traditional troubleshooting tools such as a debugger to be of little use with a Heisenbug. Sometimes brute force methods such as logging can help you identity the cause of the problem. At times all you can work with is what is known about the circumstances of failures. Stay calm and eliminate possibilities.

Mandelbug

A Mandelbug is named after Benoit Mandelbrot, the father of fractal geometry. It has behavior that appears chaotic and has complex causes, making it difficult to analyze and correct the problem. A Mandelbug may indicate the underlying system is overly complex; resolution may involve refining the design or fixing multiple areas of the software. Removing complexity and getting components to coordinately smoothly helps avoid Mandelbugs.

A Mandelbug can also refer to a bug with fractal behavior, in which a root problem leads to additional problems. For example, a bug that causes incorrect data to be stored might lead to a series of other failures because of the unexpected data. In this case, the symptoms are many and varied but there is a single root problem—which can be rapidly addressed once identified.

Schrödinbug

A Schrödinbug is a problem you didn't know you had with running software. After reviewing the source code, you realize the code should never have worked in the first place—at which point the program stops working. As odd and unlikely as this sounds, this is exactly what the perception can be. Like Schrödinger's Cat, the software is alive and dead until observed. In reality, the software may have never worked and no one noticed; or the code being examined is not the same version of the code that is running; or some factor critical to the software working has changed.

Hindenbug

A Hindenbug is a bug with catastrophic consequences, named after the Hindenburg disaster. Examples of Heisenbugs are bugs that erroneously delete precious data; bugs that cause medical equipment to malfunction; or bugs that cause aircraft to crash.

Although reproducing an issue is a common first step in debugging, it is inadvisable for this kind of bug unless you have a sure way to suppress the consequences during investigation.

Use Debuggers to Inspect Code Flow and Variables

An external view of an issue is not always sufficient to understand what's actually going wrong in the code. When a debugger is available, you can see what's going on internally by setting breakpoints, watching the flow of execution, and inspecting variables and the call stack.

Debuggers help you confirm whether a hypothesis about the cause of a failure is correct. For example, if you believe a calculation is failing due to a divide by zero error you can inspect the divisor value in a debugger before executing the calculation.

Debuggers can also help you narrow in on the source of a problem in code. For example, you may know that an error is surfacing at a certain point in your code but it may be unclear which of the underlying functions that are being called are the source of the error. By single-stepping through code and stepping over code you can rapidly exonerate entire sections of code and locate the culprit.

Web developers can take advantage of the JavaScript debuggers available in the F12 developer tools of most mainstream browsers.

Get a Second Opinion

At times, a bug investigation can take you to a place where you have no working explanation for what's going on and struggle to make progress. When you're at your wits end, what often helps is to explain the problem to someone else. The other person may have some valuable thoughts on what the problem may be, and the mere act of collecting your thoughts to walk someone else through your code often reveals a new insight.

Get a second opinion when you're struggling. Explaining a problem to someone else often results in sudden insight.

Logging

Logging is a simple mechanism you can use to output activity and errors as your application runs which can later be inspected. If you implement logging, consider carefully the errors and other information you want to log and what settings you can use to control the level of logging. It's a good idea to have a log trimming mechanism in place such that older entries get deleted from logs automatically, which is preferable to endlessly growing logs. In addition to server-side logging, JavaScript code in web pages can use *console.log* to write to the browser console.

Logging is something you can choose to provide in your application, but that isn't the only source of logging information: logging or tracing may also be available from other sources such as your operating system, web server, database server, hosting environment, development environment, and browser.

As simple as logging is, it's sometimes your most valuable diagnostic tool. When you're trying to analyze a bug which only fails in Production or in the cloud, the inability to use a debugger can really inhibit you; but logging can still be used.

Use logging to get information about errors and application state when direct debugging isn't possible.

PART III: LEARN FROM YOUR BUGS

""Don't just fix the bugs; fix whatever permitted the bugs in the first place."–Anonymous

---

The silver lining in every bug fix is what you can learn from it. Ironically, those pesky bugs that give you so much trouble are the very key to avoiding future bugs—if you pay attention to the causes and learn from them.

Chapter 8 discusses how to fix bugs completely, instead of minimally.

Chapter 9 describes the causes and remedies of many kinds of bugs.

8 FIXING BUGS COMPLETELY

"Never allow the same bug to bite you twice."
—Steve Maguire

Narrative

Jon thanked Jeff for assisting him in debugging his JavaScript problem. "Thanks for your help. I'll check this fix in and get going on my next bug," he said. "Not so fast!" said Jeff. "You've fixed your bug, but you haven't fixed it completely." Jon was caught off guard. "What do you mean, 'completely'? I've fixed the issue, and I've tested the fix. What else is there?"

"Are you sure this code change doesn't have any side effects? It's of no use to fix a problem if it creates another one." Jon spent some time looking at the code and where it was used. Finally he announced "Okay. I'm sure there's no negative impact from this change. Am I done now?"

"Not yet you're not," said Jeff. "Does this problem exist anywhere else in the code?" asked Jeff. Jon considered. "Well, I don't know. It's possible I've made the same mistake in other places." "You need to find them, fix them, and test them," said Jeff. "Go ahead—I'll wait around." Chagrined, Jon searched for other places where he might have made the same mistake. He found two other instances and corrected the code, then tested the fixes. "Okay, said Jon. Surely now I'm finished."

"One more thing," said Jeff. "This particular bug needs to never happen again. Ever. What changes are you going to put in place so that there is never a recurrence?" Jon considered, then said "I thought I was pretty good with Ajax, but I never thought about Ajax calls in the context of a loop before. I won't make this error again, and I've already fixed the code. What else is there?" "I think it would be a good idea to bolster your understanding of asynchronous patterns in Ajax," said Jeff. "I'll send you a link to some good content about that. In addition, I'd like you to share this bug and what you learned from it at our weekly developer discussion next week. The other developers could benefit from being reminded about correct asynchronous patterns."

Escaping a Chronic Bug Situation

Having a bug to fix isn't all bad news: it's also an opportunity to learn and improve. Don't make the mistake of failing to analyze your bugs as you fix them: those who fail to learn from bugs are doomed to repeat them! You'll end up with endless churn where there is lots of motion but no progress, like Sisyphus in Greek mythology who was doomed to keep rolling a boulder up a hill over and over. Instead, be like Archimedes ("give me the place to stand, and I shall move the earth"). The escape route from a chronic bug situation is changing what you do and finding the most effective levers.

Sisyphus (motion) vs. Archimedes (progress):
Don't be the guy on the left

The Elements of a Complete Bug Fix

The process of resolving a bug is simply not complete if you haven't learned something from it. You need to figure out what needs to change so that bug doesn't happen again.

Let's consider how a typical programmer bug fix goes. The developer analyzes a bug and the source code and figures out what to do about it. A fix is made, and is hopefully verified with a test. If the fix doesn't work quite as expected, the fix is re-worked and re-tested until the developer is satisfied.

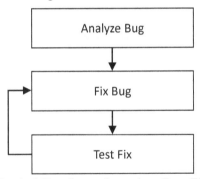

Typical Developer Steps in a Bug Fix

This is very typical—and also woefully incomplete! Each time you resolve a bug that is a real issue, ask yourself some key questions:

- Why did the bug happen?
- Does the same problem exist elsewhere?
- Does your fix introduce any new bugs, or have any negative impact on other areas of the software?
- How can you prevent a recurrence?

- What guidance / discussion with other team members is needed?

A complete bug fix is more complete and has additional steps. The testing of the fix needs to be comprehensive, to the point where you are confident you have not added new bugs or had some negative effect on other parts of the software. For example, if you modified a CSS style you should consider where else that style is used.

After verifying your fix, you need to apply the same fix any-where else it might be needed — whether you do that personally or coordinate with other developers.

Next comes learning from the bug. Consider why it happened.

Finally, you want to take steps to prevent this particular bug from ever happening again. This is where a change in quality happens.

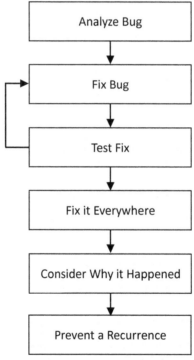

Fixing a Bug Completely

Let's expand on preventing a recurrence. What needs to change in order to prevent a bug from recurring depends on the bug. You might need to change your habits, such as reading requirements more carefully or building in more time for developer testing. You might need to improve your skills, such as understanding JavaScript better or improving how you estimate work. You might need to be more thorough in your technical design or coding. Code might need to be refactored. Someone else on your team might need to change. Whatever the needed change is, do something about it. Then share it with the rest of the team.

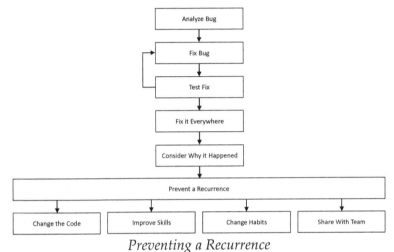

Preventing a Recurrence

When a project has high bug counts development teams can be under great pressure to quickly resolve many bugs—but this is the time when the most can be learned from them. Don't shortchange yourself with quick-but-incomplete bug fixes. Teams suffering from a large bug problem will not improve unless something changes. Look for patterns of the same problem occurring. Think about team-wide deficiencies in work habits, skills, or communication that need to be addressed.

Learn from your bugs. Drive improvements into the code, your skills, and your work habits to prevent recurrences.

Improving Weak Areas

If your bug reports include a *bug category* field, then you can do some valuable analysis. It is instructive to look at your bugs and see how many fall into each category. The categories with the largest counts indicate problem areas. Improving your skills and work habits in problem areas is a worthwhile time investment that will pay lasting dividends in the quality of your work. This is also an excellent group exercise for teams.

Analyze your bugs by category and work on improving the problem areas.

For example, imagine that a categorical analysis of your bugs revealed a distribution like the one shown below. In this case, the largest problem areas are visual problems (42%), then functional problems (14%), then interaction problems (10%). Since *visual* is the category with the most problems, start there: effort should be expended on improving your front-end developer skills and how you coordinate with the rest of your team on visual issues. When you're seeing improvement, move on to the next largest category.

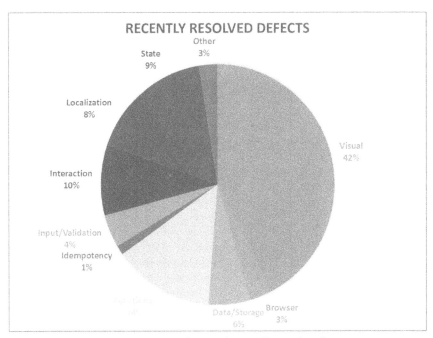

Sample Analysis of Developer Bugs by Category

9 BUG CAUSES AND REMEDIES

"When you catch bugs early, you also get fewer compound bugs. Compound bugs are two separate bugs that interact: you trip going downstairs, and when you reach for the handrail it comes off in your hand."
—Paul Graham, "The Other Road Ahead," 2001

Narrative

Jon's next meeting was the weekly developer meeting. "Several of you are having trouble resolving issues," said the development manager, "so I'd like us to discuss them as a group. Who'd like to go first?"

Brian volunteered, and put some code up on the screen. "I've been struggling to get this database update code working right all week," he said. Several developers asked questions as they pored over the code, then Ruth spoke up "I think you need to update your tables in a different or-

der. We recently made some changes and additions to the referential integrity rules." Jeff added, "Also, you could structure this code a little bit differently, which would have given you more detail about the error." Brian had the answers he needed, and thanked everyone for their help.

Next up was Pete, a front-end developer. "This is probably because I'm new to Bootstrap," he said, "but I'm having a hard time getting the pending tasks page to display correctly on different size screens. The team looked over the code, then Howie spoke up. "I think that section right there is your problem. Those style classes you've added are fighting the framework instead of letting it do the work." Howie showed some classes built into Bootstrap that Pete could be using instead. After some discussion and a few code changes, Pete had been put on the right path.

Lastly, Mahesh shared a problem he was having getting dates to display in the user's local time zone in his JavaScript code. Jon excitedly put up his hand "I think I know what the problem is—I faced the same issue recently." He proceeded to share what he had learned about quirks of the JavaScript date object and patterns he had found useful in converting between UTC time and local time. Mahesh soon had his issue resolved.

Jon felt terrific: knowledge he had learned from a past problem was now helping someone else. He reflected on how quickly these tough problems had been solved by a group effort. "We all know something about bugs and their causes," he thought to himself, "but when we put our heads together our team is an amazing knowledge base."

Bug Causes and Remedies

Understanding why a bug happened in the first place is valuable, actionable information. If you know why a problem happened, you can do something about it. In the remainder of this chapter we'll examine common bugs developers encounter, grouped by category.

As you start to learn about categories of bugs and their causes, you'll find yourself diagnosing problems faster as you recognize familiar patterns. This effect is multiplied further if the entire development team meets periodically to discuss bugs and remedies.

Arithmetic and Counting Problems

Counting problems include off-by-one errors, where your logic gets a boundary condition wrong such as the starting and ending value for loops; or from counting too few or too many items, perhaps due to an incorrect data query.

Be careful about loop boundary conditions and data queries.

Problems with calculations can be due to an incorrect understanding of requirements and formulas; or to poor implementation of the calculation. Be careful about the choice of data types to represent numbers, precision, calculation algorithms, rounding, casting, and the potential for divide by zero or overflow.

Be aware that floating point numbers inherently represent numbers with rounding—and arithmetic operations compound rounding errors. If you're skeptical that this is true, enter the following JavaScript in a web browser with the F12 developer tools console open: 0.1 + 0.2. You won't get 0.3, you'll get something along the lines of 0.30000000000000004. Similarly, 1.0 – 0.9 – 0.1 won't give you 0.0. If this comes as a shock, remember that floating point is nothing to fear as long as you understand its nature, use a sufficient number of digits for precision, and round the results of computations. Alternative representations for numbers are sometimes a better choice, such fractions or scaled integers. Floating point is not a great representation for currency, which is better represented as an integer or (in some programming languages) a decimal type.

---

*Use the right data types for what you need to repre-
sent and understand their limitations.*

Incorrect Calculations

*Computed sales tax amount is incorrect as per the documented for-
mula.*

The mortgage interest calculation is incorrect about 25% of the time.

First confirm you understand the requirements and required calculations correctly, then check the correctness of the implementation. Watch out for cumulative rounding errors in calculations in-
volving floating point numbers. Beware of values being cast to
other types during calculations, which may cause a loss of precision.

Incorrect Counts

Order count includes cancelled orders but should not.

The product report is listing products that have been deleted.

Check you are counting the right things by verifying the correctness of data queries and any code that filters a list of items. If your
database records contain an IsDeleted field, be sure your where
conditions account for that so deleted records.

Next check whether you are initializing and incrementing
counter variables correctly. Lastly, check for errors in the body of
a loop that may cause counting code to be skipped.

Off-by-One Errors

Shopping cart item count should be 3 but shows as 2.
*After checking the first item on the task list, the second item is
checked when revisiting the task list page.*

Confirm your loops have the correct starting value, increment,
and ending value. When accessing arrays and collections ensure
you are using the correct base value (such as zero or one).

Divide-by-Zero Errors

When there are no items in the shopping cart, a Divide By Zero error results when Average Savings Per Item is computed.

Never perform a division operation unless you are sure the divisor is non-zero. When the divisor is zero, use a pre-determined value or a different calculation to return a correct result. For example, if you needed to compute the average grade from a batch of student test exams you might total the grades then divide by the number of exams (sum-of-grades / number-of-exams); however when number-of-exams is zero, code can check for that condition and return zero as the average instead of performing the division.

Overflow Errors

The Mortgage Amortization Schedule crashes with an Arithmetic Overflow error when the property value amounts are in the multi-million dollar range.

An arithmetic overflow (or underflow) condition occurs when the result of a calculation is too large or small to represent. These errors can also result from casting a value from one data type to another. In 1996, the French Ariane 5 rocket crashed because its software failed to handle an overflow condition. Check the range of values in advance against what your data types can hold. Use try-catch handling around calculations you cannot be sure about and provide alternative handling in the case of an overflow. In your developer testing and unit tests, exercise the software with very large and very small values.

Rounding Problems

Interest earned calculation is off by as much as $0.15 at times.

Verify your logic is sound: are you rounding up or down, and to what number of significant digits? Make sure the variables and storage types you are using have sufficient precision. Avoid numeric approximations such as floating point numbers whenever possible and keep in mind that calculations on floating point numbers are prone to cumulative rounding errors.

Consistency Problems

In order for software to be approachable, intuitive, and highly productive consistency is essential. From user interface to behavior, consistency is what reduces learning time and eliminates surprises. Your applicant should have consistency in its user interface, behaviors, architecture, and construction.

Consistency in user interface design and behaviors may not be in a developer's control. If your product planners and visual designer are violating consistency in their designs, find a way to constructively point that out. Your solution should be consistent within itself, but also consistent with user expectations from external forces such as industry standards.

Consistency is achieved by doing things the same way and especially by centralizing code—and that includes HTML markup, CSS styles, JavaScript-code, server-side code, and database stored procedures. When you have more than one piece of code that does the same thing, you run the risk of unintended differences. The simple but profound software principle Don't Repeat Yourself (DRY) has many valuable applications: have *one* class that handles a business entity; have *one* markup view that displays a confirmation prompt; have *one* style for a dialog title.

Follow the Don't Repeat Yourself principle. Don't implement the same thing multiple times.

Inconsistent Styling

The styling of the Confirm Delete Contact dialog is different from the Confirm Update Contact dialog.

The Submit button on the Add Order dialog is green and large, but the button is blue and smaller on other dialogs.

Centralize styles for visual elements that have many instances, such as dialogs, titles, buttons, labels, and input controls. Use meaningful names, document key styles, and make sure the team is aware of them and how they are intended to be used.

Inconsistent Terminology

The styling of the Confirm Delete Contact dialog is different from the Confirm Update Contact dialog.

On the Add Task page the cancel button caption is "Cancel", but on Edit Task it is "Abandon".

Use consistent terminology. Centralize your text definitions for visual elements in a text message repository. For example, pull the "Cancel" button caption text for all your dialogs from one central definition. Also use consistent terminology in labels and help text: don't call a person a "candidate" on one screen and the same person an "applicant" on another screen.

Inconsistent Behavior

After adding a contact the form allows you to add another without leaving the page, but when adding a provider there is no option to add another.

The Import Contact wizard does not save state and always starts over at the first step, but the Import Spreadsheet wizard does save state, so that if you leave in the middle and later return you can resume where you left off.

Provide users with consistent patterns of use so they know what to expect. Consistent behaviors make software intuitive to use; inconsistent behaviors are frustrating.

Inconsistent Paradigms

The description editor strongly resembles Microsoft Word and has similar toolbars, but Ctrl+B doesn't toggle bold and Ctrl+I doesn't toggle italics.

A paradigm is pattern. Sometimes software interface design appeals to a paradigm the user is already familiar with. For example, a calendar control might be made to resemble Microsoft Outlook; or a list of search results might resemble those from a popular search engine. Problems arise when software sets this kind of expectation but then acts differently. If you appeal to a well-known paradigm, deliver on it so you don't disappoint the user.

Inconsistent Requirements

The Order Product Page requirement says shipping costs are included in an order subtotal, but the Order Confirmation Email requirement says shipping costs are not part of the order subtotal.

Requirements also need to be consistent. If Requirement A is at odds with Requirement B, the conflict needs to be resolved.

Functional Problems

Functional problems are issues where the expected functionality is not there, is not complete, or is not right. These kind of issues can arise from: a misunderstanding or miscommunication of the requirements; a flawed approach or design; an incomplete implementation; or an improper implementation.

Check your understanding of the requirements, the correctness of your approach, and the correctness of your implementation.

Missing Functionality

User is unable to remove tasks from To Do list.

Add Order page does not allow entry of a shipping address.

Approval task is not created for approver.

The only remedy to missing functionality is to create it or integrate something that already exists. If the implementation is missing, provide one. If the implementation is partial, complete it. If the implementation is flawed, correct it or replace it.

Logic Errors

The check to allow future dates is backwards. Future dates are disallowed, and past dates are accepted.

The flow of logic may be incorrect or backwards. If your logic is meant to mirror business rules dictated by your requirements, go back and compare the code against the rules. Be meticulous in testing: you need to verify that each branch of logic is working correctly.

Incorrect Functionality / Unexpected Functionality

After rearranging survey questions and saving them, when calling them up later they are not in the correct order.

Saving an incomplete feedback form for later is actually submitting the form as final.

Incorrect functionality can have several root causes. If the source of trouble is someone else's code that you depend on, get the bug reassigned to the developer who can take corrective action. If the problem is in third-party code or open source code, leverage direct support if available or community support. If the trouble is in your code, debug and correct the issue; then take steps to avoid a recurrence.

Sometimes incorrect functionality is due to an incorrect understanding of the requirements. Going forward, read requirements more carefully, and echo back your understand to the story author for confirmation that your understanding is correct and complete.

Incorrect functionality can also result from an incomplete or flawed implementation. In the future, think through problems and requirements more completely before writing code. Pitch your design and approach to a superior or peer for validation. Do better developer testing before releasing code for formal testing.

Yet another reason for incorrect functionality can be code that is out of control. Code can get out of control if it is overly complex or if its workings are unclear to the developers working on it. Once code becomes muddled, strong action is necessary to put it right. Refactor the code, or if necessary completely re-implement it. Improve your discipline, and ensure you stay in control of the code. You need well-designed classes and functions that have clear purposes, good structure, and are not overly long.

Null Reference Errors / Unexpected Values

The Favorites list fails for user jkelly. In the error log, a Null Reference Exception is logged.

When a survey form is submitted with some questions unanswered, the submit fails with a null reference exception.

In code we often get values from other functions and we also pass values on to other functions. Unless you set a variable's value yourself, it could have a null, empty, or unexpected value. If you then pass that questionable value to other functions or APIs, they can fail. Be sure you are familiar with the values used by other functions or APIs you interact with: know what they can return to you, and what they expect.

Checking for unexpected values—especially null—is vital. Code defensively. When accessing array elements, check your index against the array length before attempting to access an element. When accessing collections, check your key exists before attempting to access an item.

Improper Conditions

The appointment scheduler page is permitting appointments to be made for future dates but not for today.

The order entry taxable-item logic appears to be reversed from what the requirements state

Conditions appear all over code: they're in if statements, while statements, and database queries. It's easy to get them backwards or wrong in other ways.

One error that programmers sometimes make with if statements is having a single = instead of == to check equality. This causes an assignment instead of a comparison.

```
if (x = 5) ...          // should be if (x == 5)
```

In draft code, conditionals can also suffer from confusing < with <=, > with >=, == with <>, or extraneous/missing ! (not) operators.

Over time, conditionals in code may get extended with more conditions. Complicated conditionals quickly become unwieldy, as they involve multiple nots (!), ands (&&), ors (||), and parentheses. Code like this is easy to get wrong and can be very unclear. Therefore, since you want your code to be clean and maintainable, find ways to make intricate conditionals clearer—even if it means decomposing them or making the code slightly longer: it's worth it if it converts mystifying code into clear intent.

Error Messages / Crashes

An error message is displayed when submitting a new order.

The browser redirects to an error page when navigating to Reports.

Crashing code is never pretty. This can result from a poor implementation where the design is flawed or code structure is faulty/sloppy. It can also result from repurposed code that has unanticipated side effects and behaviors.

In addition to finding and resolving the cause of the failures, you should have a mechanism for how unexpected failures are presented to users. It's better to inform a user something has failed with understandable messages and a path to recovery than for software to crash with a highly technical error message.

Out-of-Control Code

The spell checker works unpredictably; sometimes it's fine, sometimes it misses misspelled words, and sometimes it crashes.

One of the worst things that can happen in software is when code gets out of control. This can result from:

- overly complex code or code you inherited that is murky and poorly-understood.
- code with a lack of focus, where a class or function or interface doesn't have a clear purpose and is trying to accomplish too many things.

- multiple components of code that aren't cooperating well; the components may be fine individually but the design for integrating them is faulty or not understood in the same way across the team.
- the developer doesn't know the language or frameworks or libraries they are using very well, resulting in code with unexpected side effects.

Staying in control of your code is absolutely essential. Code that is out-of-control must be tamed: either find a way to understand it and refactor it, or if necessary reimplement it altogether.

Stay in control of your code at all times. Don't tolerate murky, muddled, or mystifying behavior from software. Take the necessary action to refactor or reimplement renegade code.

Visual Problems

Visual problems include a wide range of display-related issues with the user interface.

Many visual problems are rooted in a lack of consistency. It is inherently difficult to get a consistent visual result when multiple people are working on a user interface. Meeting that objective requires a good visual design, clearly-defined style conventions and UI patterns, well-structured style rules, and consistent implementation by competent front-end developers. Even when all of those elements are present, visual problems can result as the visual design changes over time.

For web interfaces, it is very easy for CSS styles to get out of control unless they are treated in a very rigorous manner. Style rules are code, and should be treated like it: there should be meaningful names, commenting, a logical arrangement, and proper scoping. A front-end developer should never modify a style rule without fully gauging the impact that change will have across the rest of the software. Consider using a CSS pre-processor such as LESS or SASS which adds valuable features like variables and functions.

You can use online tools like csslint to review your CSS, and human reviews of the user interface and style code are also a good idea. Signs that your style rules may be out of control include multiple definitions for central elements such as h1/h2/h3; and over-use of !important and z-index.

Responsive frameworks such as Foundation or Bootstrap can offload a lot of the direct style work from developers. However, when developers have a lack of familiarity with the concepts behind a framework and its correct usage you can still end up with a mess.

Don't let style rules get out of control. Be as disciplined with style rules as you are with all other code.

Failure to Follow Visual Design Conventions

Success message should not be shown in red color.

Assign Task icon button has the wrong icon.

Ensure visual design and style conventions have been defined, and that you and other developers are acquainted with them. Then follow them. Have regular reviews with the visual designer and front-end developers and enforce your conventions. Have a set of well-named, well-designed style rules for common visual elements that everyone is acquainted with. Document your style rules and techniques.

Display Problems on Multiple Form Factors

The sales commission report is unusable on phones because the table rows wrap onto multiple lines.

The in-app documentation is unusable on phones because the type is too small to be read.

The page heading doesn't fit well on tables in portrait orientation; the right-most UI elements are not visible.

This type of bug involves markup and styles that fail to consider the range of form factors you are targeting. A screen that may look just fine at an average desktop resolution might look awkward and problematic on a phone or tablet. It's common for software projects that have a user interface to use *responsive web design*, which adapts user interfaces to support a range of device sizes from phones to desktops. Responsive web design is easy to understand but involves quite a bit of work to implement well.

Developers should be testing on a mix of screen sizes and have access to device emulators. If the first time your software was tried on a phone or tablet was by QA, it should come as no surprise that bugs are being found.

If responsive web design is a requirement for your project, front-end developers should be acquainted with responsive web design principles and follow well-defined patterns and rules. They should also be consulting regularly with your visual designer. When that's not the case, you can end up with a UI that looks fine in some sizes and awful in others.

If your project uses a framework for responsive web design, such as Bootstrap, this kind of bug can arise when developers fail to use the framework universally or correctly.

Responsive web design failure also shows up when developers use fixed units in style rules such as px or pt instead of proportional units like em and %. However, proportional units alone won't always provide attractive results: you could have visual elements that are too small to read or click on phones, or that are ridiculously oversize on large desktops. In those cases, consider using media queries to define best sizes for several classes of screen size. Responsive frameworks like Bootstrap have this idea built-in to their styles.

Even when the core fundamentals of responsive web design are being followed, there are times when a screen simply can't be rendered well on a very small device. For example, a table with 10 columns might work well on a desktop or tablet, but be impossible to render legibly on a phone. In those cases, the design ought to allow some accommodation for small-size devices. That could mean non-essential visual elements are omitted, or a different layout is used, or some elements are initially out-of-sight until summoned by the user. Visual designs often tend to go through refinement over time, so if your design fails to account for the realities of the device sizes you need to work with you should request the design be reviewed and improved. Ideally your visual designer will be following a *mobile-first* approach, where you begin with the small device experience first to ensure it is usable and fully-functional rather than treating it as an afterthought.

If you or your fellow developers are unsure about responsive web design, get up to speed as quickly as possible through an online learning course, books, or mentorship. Connect to developer support forums on responsive web design where you can ask questions.

Ensure you have well-defined responsive web design rules and that they are being followed consistently.

Missing, Improper, or Inconsistent Visual Cues

Hand cursor does not appear over download icon.

Zoom icon is missing tooltip.

Assign Task icon button has the wrong icon.

Visual cues provide users with certainty as they explore your application. Follow your style conventions. If style conventions are incomplete, get consensus on additional details and expand them. Follow the DRY principle and avoid duplication in style rules.

Inconsistent Labels, Captions, Titles, Fonts, Colors

Cancel button caption is "Close" on some dialogs and "Cancel" on others.

Follow your style conventions. If style conventions are incomplete, get consensus on additional details and expand them. Follow the DRY principle and avoid duplication in style rules.

Container Size Problems

Dialog height is insufficient for all controls to be visible.

When the notes sidebar contains a large note not all of it can be read.

Ensure your content containers (pages, dialogs, panels, sidebars) have well-reasoned and intentional sizing: are they fixed in size or proportional? Do they provide scrolling when their content exceeds the size of the container? Test your user interface across the spectrum of screen sizes you intend to support.

Layout, Spacing, and Alignment Problems

Help and Close icons are misaligned vertically.

Title is left-aligned on the Help dialog but centered on all other dialogs.

Show Only My templates checkbox is not positioned within the Options panel.

Spacing around footer does not match visual design comp.

There is a space missing between check box and text.

A UI with layout, spacing, and alignment problems screams "this software is unfinished" to a user. Follow your style conventions. If style conventions are incomplete, get consensus on additional details and expand them. Follow the DRY principle and avoid duplication in style rules. The more you can centralize how layout, spacing, and alignment are controlled the more consistency you'll have.

Partial Visibility

In the Calendar control, the last week of the month is off the screen.

Unable to see the complete report title.

The pop-up menu is not completely visible.

Partial visibility problems can be caused by visual elements whose position or size is incorrect, or are set to a fixed size that doesn't render well on all screen sizes. Use responsive web design techniques, including proportional units and media queries to accommodate different size screens.

Partial visibility can also result from text that is longer than the allotted area. Options include giving the text a larger area to render in; reducing font size; reducing the text itself to be shorter; or showing partial text followed by an ellipsis (...).

Another possible cause of partial visibility is a z-index problem, where the top-most elements of the display are not the intended elements. Review your style rules that set z-index. Third-party controls may also be setting z-index.

Style Rule Conflicts

Navigation bar is not highlighted in the expected color.

The sidebar panel has an incorrect font.

CSS stands for <u>Cascading</u> Style Sheets, and it's the cascading that's at the heart of many style rule conflicts. Style rules are very powerful, but they also require discipline. The average web application has many style rules in many places—and a shortage of discipline.

A clear sign that rules are in conflict, besides the visual evidence, is when you have rampant use of !important throughout your style rules. Nine times out ten, when !important is used by a developer it should not be—it solves the immediate problem but triggers more problems. You can use the F12 developer tools built into most browsers to study how your rules cascade.

The answer is to scope style rules properly:

1. Think through your style rules and document how they are meant to be used, including how they are meant to be combined. Rules should cascade in an orderly way, not an accidental way.
2. Ensure each of the rules have correct selectors—not too broad and not too narrow.
3. Apply the rules to HTML elements in a way that is consistent with the guidance you created in Step 1.

This sounds simple, but in practice it is not—especially when there are multiple people writing style rules on a team.

Browser Problems

Browser problems include compatibility problems, where there is undesirable behavior exhibited by one particular browser. In your web code, stick to standard, widely-accepted HTML features, CSS features, and JavaScript features. Use an online validator to check your code. If you must use a feature that is not generally available, include checks for the feature and fall back to an acceptable alternative behavior when it is not available. When you encounter browser compatibility issues with open source libraries and commercial libraries, check your community and support channels for a known solution or work-around, or post a question.

Wherever possible, stick to mainstream web features that are well-supported across browsers and have strong community support.

Browser problems can also arise from caching. Under-caching means unnecessary web traffic and poor performance, whereas over-caching can cause out-of-date content to be shown to users. You should leverage caching, but stay in control of it. If you use far future expiration dates to keep content cached, also have a strategy for handling content updates such as including a content version number in the URL. Placing content in a Content Delivery Network (CDN) can speed up performance regardless of user location, but you'll similarly need to balance content expiration with how you handle updated content.

Use an effective caching strategy but stay in control
of it and have a means for updating content.

A web developer should not fall into the trap of just using one preferred browser. Rotate between different browsers regularly. Speaking of which, if you haven't formally identified which browsers you are supporting you should get that defined without delay. The same goes for mobile devices. Be sure to test your code on supported browsers and devices.

Know which browsers you are targeting. Rotate the
browsers you use, and do developer testing on the
same browsers that QA is testing on.

Different Appearance or Behavior on One Browser

Form labels do not align in Internet Explorer 11 only.

Dragging items does not work in Firefox.

Avoid using features that are not supported by all of your target browsers; or check for the existence of features and have a fallback behavior when they are not available.

For checking whether a browser supports a feature, it's best to check for availability of the feature—not the browser type/version. The Modernizr library can be very useful in detecting which features are available in a user's browser.

Browser Rendering Differences

Internet Explorer is rendering the page in "quirks mode".

Safari and Firefox draw a border around empty table calls and other browsers do not.

Chrome is not displaying background color on some div elements.

Some browsers are not rendering canvas elements.

Ensure you have a valid <!DOCTYPE...> element at the top of your HTML. For HTML5, this is simply <!DOCTYPE html>. When a DOCTYPE declaration is not present, different browsers may make different assumptions about the version of HTML you are targeting. If a browser believes a page has less-than-ideal HTML, it can enter quirks mode automatically and result in unexpected page rendering. If you are unsure whether a page is rendering in quirks mode, you can go to your F12 developer tools JavaScript console on most browsers and inspect document.compatMode.

Browser is Showing Out-of-Date Items

Data displayed is not current unless I clear browser cache.

Dated versions of images appear in the browser even though the images have been updated.

Over-caching can cause out-of-date content to appear in your web application. Have a deliberate caching strategy to reduce unnecessary web traffic that includes setting content expiration dates and leveraging a CDN. Be sure you have a method for handling updated content, such as including a content version number in URLs.

Browsers Render Default Fonts, Margins, etc. Differently

On IE, the page has a significantly different margin from other browsers.

On Chrome, text boxes have yellow borders.

Use a CSS Reset stylesheet to ensure a standard baseline across all browsers before applying your own style rules. Specify style rules for all of the layout and font details you care about.

Vendor-specific CSS not Rendering Consistently

Opacity setting is honored in Firefox and Internet Explorer but not Chrome or Safari.

Ensure all vendor prefixes are represented in your CSS styles. Use a reference site or online validation tool to check correctness. If you use LESS or SASS, consider using mix-ins to apply vendor prefixes.

Page is Broken on Some Browsers

Page renders only partially on Internet Explorer.

Ensure your HTML and CSS are valid. Check for missing elements, improperly nested elements, missing/extra angle brackets, and misspellings. Use an online validation tool to check your code.

Mobile Problems

In addition to all of the issues that can happen in the *visual* category, mobile devices require additional handholding for a satisfactory experience. Software that needs to work on mobile devices should not assume the user has very much screen real estate, or a mouse that can hover. Screen designs for small devices should avoid having multiple scrollable areas.

Interactive elements should be sized and spaced such that they can be touched with accuracy. A fingertip is much larger than a mouse cursor. Visual elements smaller than 44 x 44 pixels or less than 8 pixels apart are challenging to touch.

Improper Rendering

Form layout wraps exceedingly on phone-sized devices.

Panel is larger than phone width.

Font size is too small to read.

Web apps today can be consumed on a wide variety of devices with screens large and small. When form layout does not render acceptably on some kinds of mobile device or there are size problems, this indicates a failure to design responsively. Follow the principles of *responsive web design* to create pages and styles that render well on any size device.

- Use a flexible grid system to divide your page into proportional areas.
- Use relative units for fonts and layout (such as % and em) rather than absolute units.
- When you need different layouts for different classes of device, use CSS media queries to adapt layout.

Consider using a responsive framework such as Bootstrap of Foundation which leverage all of the above techniques.

Cannot Access Tooltips or Rollover on Mobile Device

Cannot access icon tooltips on phone.

There is no way to get rollover displays on a tablet.

On a mobile device without a mouse, there are no hover events. To give mobile users access to functionality such as tooltips, provide an equivalent click event so mobile users have a way to get to tooltips and rollovers.

Functionality Not Working on Mobile Devices

Video cannot be played on mobile devices because their browsers disallow Flash.

A technology that works fine on the desktop may not be available on some mobile devices. For example, Adobe Flash is not supported on most mobile devices. Avoid technology dependencies that are not available on all of the device platforms you plan to support; instead, use widely supported standards such as HTML5 audio and video standards. If you must use a technology that is not widely supported, then implement a fallback technology for mobile devices.

Unable to Access Full Functionality from Mobile Device

Unable to access administration features from my phone even though I am signed in as an admin.

The mobile app doesn't have the manage documents feature.

It's best not to limit content or available functionality based on device size. Ideally, you want your mobile device user to have full use of your application. The best mobile experiences come from a *mobile-first* design approach, where the mobile device user experience is considered first, not as an afterthought. This ensures everything that can be done in the software can be done on a mobile device.

Some screen layouts that work well for desktops simply aren't effective on a small device. Rather than leaving out functional areas or visual elements that are hard to fit on a mobile device, explore an alternative layout that works on a small device without limiting what the user can do. You can use CSS media queries to switch to the most appropriate layout for a particular class of device.

Pages Display Slowly on Mobile Devices

The user profile page comes up very slowly on phones when there is an avatar picture.

The end-of-month report takes a very long time to load on phones and tablets.

If you are using full-size high-density images, you are wasting memory and increasing download time. Scale down images for mobile devices, since you can't take advantage of full-resolution images on a small screen.

Ensure your web pages are efficient. Employ minification, bundling, and caching to reduce the size of content and the amount of HTTP requests needed to retrieve it. Use profiling tools such as Yahoo's YSlow or Google PageSpeed Insights to analyze the efficiency of web pages and get tips for optimization.

Interaction Problems

There are forms and there are forms. Getting interaction right for complex forms with many moving parts can be very difficult. You may be dealing with changing form state, elements that are sometimes visible/invisible, expanding/collapsing areas, and one or more levels of pop-up dialogs.

To keep your form code from getting out of control, it's absolutely essential to have a well-designed interaction model. Start with a conceptual model that reflects the requirements and confirm it is correct and complete; then move on to a code implementation. The closer your implementation faithfully reflects the model in its structure the better off you'll be.

For complex forms, have a well-designed interaction model and use it to guide your code implementation

---

For web interfaces, there are many frameworks available such as AngularJS, Backbone, Knockout, and Ember that can assist in building rich, responsive interactions through the use of data models, templates and markup declarations. Although they have similarities, each framework is its own animal. Whether it's a good idea or not to use a framework very much depends on its nature and whether the developers know how to use it: you don't want to end up with code that is baffling to the very people who have to maintain it. Some frameworks literally take over control of your form, while others are more supplementary in the services they provide. When you do use frameworks, be sure they are well-understood and are being used properly. Any code that results in potentially-mystifying automated behaviors needs to be well-commented.

Don't use an interaction framework unless you are proficient in it. Take the mystery out of magical automatic behaviors with well-documented code.

Lack of Visual Feedback or User Confirmation

No visual confirmation when user clicks action button.

Long delay after clicking button before display updates.

When a user clicks an interaction element such as a button or link, they should get near-immediate visual feedback to acknowledge their action—otherwise they'll form doubts and start clicking again. When the software's response to a user interaction requires some waiting time, always provide some visual feedback such as a wait indicator.

Left-over or Incorrect Values in Input Fields

When returning to the Task page, the previously entered search text is still present in the search box

Part of your interaction model should cover initializing and resetting the values of input fields; failure to do this completely can leave unwanted left-over values. What's in your input fields should be intentional, not accidental.

Focus Problems

After selecting an item, the edit item dialog doesn't set focus to an input field.

Setting initial focus on a page to an input control or action button smooths the way for user interaction. Failure to set proper focus on initial page load can mean there is no code to set focus, or the focus code targets the incorrect element, or the focus code runs too early; if using jQuery, the document ready function is a good place to set focus.

Not Scrolling to End of List

After adding a new comment to a discussion, the newly added comment is not visible in the scrollable comment list.

When you have a list or other visual element that is scrollable, there are times when you want the end of the list in view. For example, just after adding a new item it's a good idea to scroll the final item into view so the user sees the item they just added. In a web interface, this can often be accomplished by using jQuery to set the scrollTop property of an element.

Visual Element Not Performing

The sidebar collapse button fails to hide the sidebar panel.

Selecting the Sales YTD Chart view option fails to display a chart.

When you have a visual element that fails to perform the desired behavior, check that you have wired up the visual element to respond to the interaction. For example, a button in a web interface needs a click handler. Then check the code that responds to the interaction for correctness. Interaction code should have error handling so that in the instance of a failure you don't leave the user hanging without a response.

Expected UI Element Fails to Appear or Disappear

Clicking on Documents icon fails to display Documents dialog.

Dialog stays present after close box is clicked.

Search results are not visible after clicking Search button.

Visual elements that fail to appear or disappear during interactions can result when their properties are not being set and updated properly. In a web interface, improper values in CSS properties such as display, visibility, opacity, or z-index can cause these kinds of symptoms. A second possibility is JavaScript code that is failing to execute or jQuery code with an improper selector.

Unexpected Visuals During Interaction

Selecting a list item unexpectedly displays a message about the selected item at the bottom of the screen.

After clicking Submit, an unexpected alert box displays.

Unexpected visuals that arise from interactions may be left-over debug aids the developer forgot to remove. When you're developer testing an interactive part of the UI, do a careful visual inspection and remove left-over visuals.

Incorrect Enabling/Disabling of Visual Elements

In the Add New Provider wizard, when moving back to step 2 from step 3 the Next button is disabled.

After clicking Submit and waiting for processing, the Submit button is still enabled and can be clicked.

The Product Category carousel's previous and next buttons are always enabled, even when on the first or last item in the list.

When you have a visual item that can be enabled or disabled at times, have a clear design for what events change its state and code it cleanly. Complex form interactions can lead to messy code to update visual elements; refactor "leaky" code until it is simple, centralized, and crisp.

When you are providing navigation controls for a list of items, such as a carousel control, disable the previous button at the top of the list and the next button at the bottom of the list, unless your intention is to allow circular cycling through the list.

Cooperative Visual Elements Fail to Cooperate

In Contact List, after setting a Filter the list of contacts is not filtered as expected.

After dragging an order to the Expedited Orders list panel, the wrong order appears in the list.

When interactions with one element of your form fail to trigger cooperative behavior by another element on the form, it may be due to a missing interaction handler, a mismatch in how the elements communicate selection data, or a flawed implementation in the handler code. Check that each component is doing its job, and that the way the components interact and cooperate with each other is soundly designed.

Interactions Possible That Should be Disabled

After clicking Submit and awaiting completion of processing, it is still possible to revise input and interact with other controls on the form.

When dragging to rearrange dashboard tiles, the controls on the tiles can still be interacted with.

When a control such as a Submit button has been clicked and further interaction with the form's controls is unwanted, be sure to disable the input controls. How many times have you ordered something online and seen a dire warning to "only click the submit button once"? Don't depend on the user to do the right thing; make it impossible to do the wrong thing.

Form Fails to Reset

Unable to add a second comment without closing and returning to form.

After entering the first contact, the input fields are not reset for the second contact.

When a form permits repetitive operations, such as adding multiple items, the form needs to be "reset" to a fresh state for each new round of data entry. Set initial values for all input fields and visibility of action controls and message areas. Forms that end up in an odd state usually lack centralized code to reset the form. Call the same initialization code when the form first loads and when readying for the next round of data entry.

Spelling and Grammatical Errors

Spelling and grammar come easily to some, but not so easily to others. This common problem has gotten even worse with today's distributed teams where not everyone is working in their first language. Even good spellers can end up with mistakes because they're typing too quickly. It's important to get spelling and grammar right, as some users will make quality judgments about software when they see errors. A generated email message with spelling or grammatical errors will often be suspected of fraudulent origin. It's not difficult to check spelling or grammar, so you should be in the habit of doing so. If you're really challenged in this area, get someone to check your work in a buddy review.

It's easy to see why this is important in the parts of software that are visible to users, but what about the internals? Does it matter if you have properly spelled names for classes, functions, parameters, variables, and database tables? It does matter. Nothing is more frustrating than not being able to find a software asset because it is spelled improperly. In dynamic languages like JavaScript, differences in spelling or case might mean you are not referring to the variable or object you think you are. For the same reason, there should be consistency in the use of upper/lower case.

Take spelling and grammar seriously. Failure to do so can result in both perceived and actual quality issues.

Improper Spelling and Grammar

The word "favorites" is misspelled as "favorits" on the Documents page.

The order confirmation email message contains the incorrect sentence "Thank for your order.".

In the code, the parameter name cutofDate should be cutoffDate.

The database table "AprovedOrders" should be "ApprovedOrders".

Include a review of spelling and grammar in your developer testing. Take advantage of online tools, or have your work reviewed by another. It you retrieve your on-screen text messages from a central repository (common in multiple language support), have someone with good spelling and grammar review all of the messages.

Inconsistent Casing

Some screens have all words in the title capitalized; others only capitalize the first word.

The Contacts data entry form has some labels capitalized and some not.

The "customer" table does not start with a capital letter like all of the other tables.

Inconsistent casing has many of the same consequences as improper spelling. Consistency makes users more comfortable and reduces surprises for programmers. Establish capitalization rules for titles, labels and messages displayed to users. Decide on where you will use camelCasing or PascalCasing for programming names and database artifacts. If your programming language already has a strongly-established convention for casing, it's best to honor it.

Inconsistent Pluralization

The database table name Order doesn't match the pluralization of table OrderItems.

Pluralization is another area where inconsistency makes it harder for a team to work together. Do you think it's better to pluralize database table names (Customers, Orders) or not (Customer, Order)? What's most important is that you select a convention and stick to it. A mixture will be confusing.

Input Validation Problems

Input validation is about providing a logical and helpful data entry experience. Validation can be applied both to individual input fields and also to a group of input fields. For example, a credit card validation would involve not only the credit card number but also the cardholder name and expiration date.

Input validation is also about protection. Good validation protects the user from making mistakes, and also protects the system from input that is incomplete, erroneous, or hostile. Even a minor oversight in validation can pollute your system with unexpected values that can cause trouble. Whether you perform validation with discrete code or employ a validation framework, it's important that your validation be both correct and complete. Unit testing with a healthy spectrum of input values is recommended.

Treat input validation as defensive points of entry into your solution.

In web solutions, you have the choice of doing validation right in the web page and/or in the server code. Doing validation on the web page can help avoid a trip to the server until the input is right; however, failure to also validate on the server exposes a major security risk because you can't know that a web request really came from your web page. For this reason, server code should always perform validation even if the web page is also performing validation. As a general rule, validation needs to be considered whenever data is passing from one tier to another; and especially when an untrusted tier is involved.

In web solutions and other client/server solutions, the server should never delegate validation to the client.

Invalid Characters Accepted for Data Type

The age field allows not only digits but also decimal point and minus sign.

The zip code field accepts letters and digits.

Entering a text comment that contains ampersand (&) causes an error message on submit.

Input fields that are too permissive can result in values that are not valid for their underlying data type. Invalid characters can cause an assortment of problems to the various tiers of your solution, so you need to prevent them from getting past your outer defenses. If possible, filter out unwanted characters right in the input field itself. For example, HTML5 web pages can filter input boxes for common data types including numbers, dates, times, and email addresses. When passing characters from web client to web server, consider that characters with special meanings in URLs may need encoding, escaping, or special handling.

Failure to Collect All Required Information

The Order Payment page allows the user to proceed without having entered a credit card number.

The registration page is not requiring an email address but is supposed to.

Always be sure to have collected all the information you need before attempting any processing. If you are defaulting values not explicitly entered, it's usually a good idea to make that clear to the user.

Requiring Optional Information

The Registration form won't accept an empty middle name, but some registrants don't have a middle name.

The page won't proceed without entry of a phone number, but that is not information the system uses in any way.

Over-zealous validation can be as bad as incomplete validation. Don't require information that you don't need, or that realistically isn't always available.

Script Injection and SQL Injection Vulnerability

The Employee table was lost after a form submit where the Last Name field was entered as: Smith'; DROP TABLE Employee;

Input containing <script> tags is being accepted; on the page where the input is re-displayed, the script is executing.

A common failure in validation logic is to only consider the intended use of the input. For example, a text comment field might be accepted with nearly any kind of value since a comment is free-form text. However, that input data also passes through a number of places in the software where certain values in the input can have an alarming effect depending on the context where it is used. Certain values in input could potentially add parameters to a web request; change what a database query does; or render script code in a web page when the data is re-displayed. For this reason, you should be in the habit of validating all input, and systematizing the ways you validate. Validate input not only for its intended use, but for safety in all contexts it will pass through.

Software that constructs database queries based on user input can be susceptible to clever input attacks where the input causes unwanted database behavior such as dropping tables. Find secure alternatives to dynamic SQL that are not susceptible to scripting attacks, such as using SQL parameters.

Web software that stores input such as text comments can be vulnerable to scripting attacks if it doesn't filter out input that contains <script> elements. When this kind of input is accepted and stored and later re-displayed, the attacker's JavaScript code can become part of the page and execute. Always filter out unwanted special characters from input, and consider all of the tiers the input data will pass through.

Failure to Transform Input Data for Processing

Adding a contact fails when the name O'Malley is entered.

Submitting the feedback form fails if the comments including an ampersand (&) character.

Input data that is perfectly valid for its intended business use can still cause troubles during processing. For example, SQL queries constructed from input data may run into problems if data values contain apostrophes. Similarly, ampersand characters can cause confusion when passed in a web request if they are interpreted as a URL query parameter separator. Transform special characters in input values that can disrupt your processing, by quoting them or encoding them.

Out-of-Sight Validation Messages

Validation error message appears on area of screen not visible to user unless they scroll to it

On long forms, the validation messages from an attempted submit may be on parts of the form not visible to the user. For example, if a user clicks submit at the bottom of a long form and validation errors are displayed near the top of the form, they won't be visible. The user shouldn't have to scroll to learn that there are validation messages. A better experience is to automatically scroll the topmost validation error into view.

Localization Problems

Software localization can be done to different levels of completeness. Although many of the traditional problems with localization have been solved by the widespread use of Unicode, localization can still be viewed as a collection of problems to solve which range from simple to nuanced to frustrating.

Common first-level localization considerations include using resource lists of strings in each supported language and supporting localized formats for dates, numbers, and currency. Don't make assumptions about word order in messages and avoid concatenating strings: "red pencil" is "crayon rouge" in French. More nuanced localization considerations include handling pluralization, case, and collation properly. Supporting languages with right-to-left order requires an extra level of implementation.

To handle localization well, don't just consider language but also locale: French in France is different from French in Canada. When handling language, date/number/currency formats, and time zone you'll need to consider which of those are determined by the user's profile in your software vs. what you can determine from the browser or operating system.

It's hard to get language support right without access to someone who can verify correctness. Although online translation tools are useful for setting up placeholder messages in other languages, they need to be reviewed and edited by a fluent speaker before putting anything in front of an actual user.

Failure to Localize Text

Label "Last name" is not localized.

Error message "Expiration date is required" is not localized.

One of the first tasks in localization is to replace hard-coded text strings with values taken from a resource list, and then to maintain resource lists for each supported locale/language. This needs to apply to all text, including menu items, titles, labels, input watermarks, tooltips, messages, and error messages. Since it's easy to miss areas in need of localization, developer testing should including localization testing.

Word Order Problems

"Blue Diamond" is displaying as "Bleu Diamant" for French users, but French speakers would actually say "Diamant Bleu".

The "missing amount" error message has incorrect word order in Spanish. It should be "cantidad que falta".

It is very easy for developers to make assumptions about word order that simply aren't universal. Localized software should never concatenate strings. How then do you handle the need to combine strings and data values, such as "5 items in your shopping cart"? A good method is to embed parameters in your localized string resources that get replaced, as in "{item-count} items in your shopping cart" in English which would become "Sepetinizde {item-count} ürün" in Turkish.

Pluralization Problems

The "0 items in your shopping cart" message in French should not be pluralized.

The "Total of x accounts" message on the Accounts Report is not pluralized correctly in Polish when x is 12-14.

Different languages have varying rules for whether pluralization requires changes in words. For example, English and German have one form for 1 and another form for other numbers, as in "1 page" vs. "2 pages". Having one string resource for singular counts and another for plural counts might seem like the right answer, but as your scope of supported languages expands a more elaborate scheme will be needed. French and Brazilian Portuguese have one form for 0, 1 and another form for other numbers; Arabic has six different forms; and Chinese and Japanese have the same form for all numbers. Languages such as Polish and Arabic have complex pluralization rules for different ranges of numbers. Don't back yourself into a corner with an overly-simplistic scheme for handling pluralization. The Unicode Common Locale Data Repository Project has defined a useful set of pluralization rules with these categories: zero, one, two, few, many, other.

Gender Problems

The "n {items} were updated" message frequently has an incorrect verb in Polish.

Language support requires proper handling of gender. English has three gender options for pronouns (male, female, and neutral), but Polish has five. A resource string pattern such as "{item-name} was added" will not work in some languages because the verb changes based on the noun. To reduce challenges in software language translation with gender, use resource strings in a known context. Avoid concatenation of strings, and avoid injecting too many dynamic values into messages.

Data Not Sorting in Expected Order

The customer list is not sorting properly in Icelandic.

English-language programmers often sort lists for display using simple comparisons. This works because the English alphabet collates in the same order as character codes are arranged in the ASCII/ANSI/Unicode character sets. However, this won't work for most other languages: in Icelandic, the *eth* (Ð) character should come between D and E. Your development environment, operating system, or database may provide features for collating by locale that you can take advantage of; if not, it's up to you to implement proper collating for your target locales. If you do sorting in more than one tier of your application, be sure you are handling sort order consistently.

Right-to-Left Order Problems

The menu options for Arabic have left-to-right text but should be right-to-left.

Some languages render their characters right-to-left, and the proper way to handle this for your user interface and text direction to mirror what you do for left-to-right languages—but there will be exceptions for some visual elements such as images, icons and clocks which will not reverse. Overcoming your natural language direction bias is difficult because it is deeply ingrained. Start with localization guidance for your development platform and take advantage of what's already available. Web applications can leverage the HTML5 *dir* directive which specifies the base direction for the page or element.

Localized Text Doesn't Fit in Available Display Area

The "Please re-enter your credit card number" message is only partially visible in German.

A short message in one language can be quite long in another. Avoid assumptions about message size, and make message areas flexible in size.

Data/Storage Problems

Data problems involve the correctness of information such as what is displayed to the user. Data problems also intersect with security problems. Sensitive data needs to be guarded so it is not compromised.

Storage problems involve correct storage and retrieval of data. Your code needs to move between logical objects and the entities your data storage supports harmoniously. Some developers favor object-relational mapping solutions to achieve this, while others much prefer to use business objects and data helper classes. The path data follows from web client to server to data storage and back again needs to be solid. This is something like a relay race, where handing off data from one place to the next must be done with great care. One weak link in the chain will compromise everything.

Treat data like the precious cargo it is. Map the path of data end-to-end and ensure there is a careful hand- off from tier to tier.

To ensure sets of related data records are stored reliably and consistently, the traditional answer has been to use relational da- tabases and *transactions*; however, in modern times the rise of cloud-based distributed solutions has led to experimentation with other approaches, such as NoSQL databases and *eventual con- sistency*. Whether you use old-school or newer techniques for stor- age and consistency, be sure you have an approach that satisfies your requirements and works reliably; and be sure to implement it fully and correctly.

Too Much, Too Little, or Incorrect Data Displayed

The Open Opportunities report should only show open opportunities owned by the current user, but is actually showing all open opportuni- ties.

When software shows incorrect data, that can result from logic errors, improper authorization checks, or incorrect data queries. Verify the logic is correct in deciding what data should be shown, including any authorization checks about what the user is entitled to view. Next confirm the data query implementation is correct. In SQL queries, check the correctness of column names, *where* and *join* clauses, use of *and/or*, and handling of null values. For exam- ple, if you have too few restrictions in a *join* clause you will prob- ably end up with more records than you bargained for.

Data Not Stored or Not Stored Properly

Order is not saved after it is submitted.

Reservation changes are only partially saved after editing.

Failure to store data can be due to logic errors, problems passing data between layers, or to implementation flaws in any of the layers. Review the flow of data across all tiers: correct mismatches between client requests and server code, and between server code and database. Check for correctness of field names.

Data Stored That Should Not Be

Review comments are saving even though user has not performed a save action.

The web site login page remembers my identity even though I never clicked Remember Me.

If your design calls for a user to perform an explicit save or submit action in order to commit data, be sure data storage is only triggered under the expected circumstances. Storing data without user consent is a trust violation, and may lead to consequences that are unwanted, embarrassing or even illegal.

Data Storage Fails with Long Values

Contact is not saved if last name > 20 characters entered.

Add code to check that maximum sizes of underlying storage (such as a column in a database table) are not being exceeded.

Data Storage Fails with Certain Characters

Unable to submit form when comments contain ampersand (&) or angle bracket (<>) characters.

Unable to store last name that includes an apostrophe such as O'Malley.

Special characters need special handling, and this is especially true on web sites. Encode special characters as needed between client and server. Use parameters rather than dynamic SQL when passing values to the database.

Data Storage Fails with International Characters

Unable to submit form when comments contain international characters.

After saving a contact with French accent characters in the name, recalling the contact changes the accent characters to other characters.

The advent of Unicode has done away with many of the legacy problems in supporting international characters, but not all of them. For data storage to work well with international characters, be sure you have <u>end-to-end</u> Unicode support. That should include fonts, UI controls, third-party software components, the programming languages you use, and underlying storage mechanisms. You should also be aware that the days are long past when a character could be represented as an 8-bit ASCII byte. Use Unicode-savvy software mechanisms and understand that a text string only makes sense if it also has a known encoding (such as UTF-8). Include international characters in your developer testing and unit tests.

Data Lifetime Problems

A document was deleted, but a search for document text is finding results from the deleted document.

Periodically the event log in the cloud database grows so large that the database reaches its maximum size.

The lifetime of data is an often-neglected but important consideration. Keeping data around longer than you need to can increase costs (especially with cloud-based storage) and leave you with a larger-than-necessary database. On the other hand, deleting data too soon can deprive users of information they need.

Design a data lifetime model for your business entities and other data artifacts (define what events create, modify, and delete them). Enforce archiving or removal of expired data in the application. Have processes in place that regularly remove older records from logs to keep them from endlessly growing.

Lastly, consider whether you ever really want to hard delete anything. Some systems are designed such that a delete is only a soft delete, where deleting a record only sets a delete flag but it is not physically removed. Although this approach allows you to recover from accidental deletion, it comes with some responsibilities: you must include a condition for the delete flag in every single data query. You also have to deal with the larger databases that result from never truly deleting records.

Data Import / Export / Conversion Problems

The Import Contacts from Spreadsheet operation only imported 17 of the 20 records in the spreadsheet.

Imported names containing apostrophes (like O'Hara) end up as O''Hara in the output.

Imported records end up with some data in the wrong fields.

When information is converted from one form to another, conversion code needs to be up to the task or data loss/mangling can result. Both the input format and output format need to be correctly and fully implemented. Consider all of the possible forms input data may take.

Some data formats are simple and some are amazingly complex. If the format you're working with is not trivial, it's usually wise to find a code library that converts the format reliably. Markup formats such as XML are frequently processed using library functions.

Many input formats have special or reserved characters. Formats such as comma-separated values or tab-separated values use a delimiter character to separate fields of data and newline to indicate end of record. With delimited data, you need to account for the possibility of the delimiter character itself appearing in the data, else the mapping of data to fields will be wrong. For example, in comma-separated values a FullName field might contain the value "John Smith, Jr. ", where you don't want the comma to be misinterpreted as the start of a new field. Consult the rules for the format you are using. Special characters in data formats are generally handled in one of these ways:

1. Embed the field value in quotation marks, as in "John Smith, Jr." to handle a comma in the data.

2. Precede the special character with an escape character, as in \" to indicate a quotation mark as data.
3. Double the special character, as in Gerald O''Malley to treat an apostrophe as data.

Use input and output tally counts as a check of the conversion process, and log errors. Test conversion code with a good spectrum of sample data.

Data Removal Causes Problems with Related Data

After deleting vendor X, attempts to access products from vendor X result in vendor record not found errors.

Disallow removal of data that other data is dependent on. Remove related records in an optimal order, such as deleting child records before the parent record. If your database supports referential integrity, make use of it to enforce proper order of removal. Consider using transactions when removing groups of related records. Delete records in a careful order based on their relationship.

Data Ends Up in Wrong Environment

Submitting an order on the QA environment caused emails to be sent to Production users

After adding a new purchase order, it is not shown in the Purchase Order Report.

Most software projects involve multiple environments. For example, you might have a development environment you work in, a QA environment for formal testing, and a Production environment for end users. When applications unexpectedly have crossover problems to other environments, major problems can ensue: data ends up in the wrong places, and it can be extremely difficult to untangle—especially if not immediately detected. One reason for environment cross-over is incorrect application configuration settings when an app is deployed to an environment, pointing for example to a database in another environment.

It's crucial that you keep your environments well-separated, especially Production. Put deployment procedures and policies in place that guard against accidental cross-over of environments:

having strong walls of separation in place is best. Never share Production servers, cloud accounts, databases, or credentials with other environments. Use strong, unique production credentials and keep them a closely-guarded secret.

Keep the production environment and credentials isolated from other environments.

Data Ends Up in Wrong Tenant

The inventory report is showing SKUs from another company.

Users are able to access documents belonging to other companies.

Software-as-a-Service (SaaS) applications support multiple tenants (organizations) with shared resources. Cross-over of data to the wrong tenant is serious and can result in a loss of business and legal troubles.

There are several SaaS models for handling tenant data. At one end of the spectrum is *separate databases*, where there is a separate database for each tenant with separate access credentials. This approach avoids many data cross-over problems, but the application must connect to the correct database for each user.

At the other end of the spectrum is *shared database, shared schema*, where a single database contains all tenant data. In this approach, records contain a tenant Id to identify which tenant a record belongs to. The application must take great pains to keep tenant data isolated. Data disclosure and cross-over storage problems can result if some database queries fail to specify the tenant Id. Centralizing data access code is recommended. Consider encryption of records with tenant-specific keys, which can reduce the damage from data access errors.

Regardless of which model you use, a means of keeping tenant data isolated is a necessity. A strong suite of multi-tenancy tests is essential.

---

*Keep tenant data isolated, either physically or
through encryption.*

State Problems

State is the data that represents the present condition of something. State can mean temporary internal state, such as variables that track the current state of an input form; or persistent state, such as the status of order records in a database. If you end up with unexpected state, software can act very unpredictably.

Some languages like JavaScript allow you keep state in global variables, which is generally considered a bad practice because more than one code component might use the same global name, resulting in unexpected behavior. It's far safer to keep state in scoped objects.

State can get out hand due to sloppy implementation, or when the requirements change so much that the original code is no longer up to the task. The key to maintaining state properly is to model it well then implement the model. Consider a state machine approach, with state variables that may have several possible values. A transition occurs when an event causes actions to execute and changes one or more state variables. For example, if you were modeling a turnstile for a subway you would have a turnstile state that could be set to locked or unlocked. The state would change to *unlocked* after a valid token is put in the slot; and would return to *locked* after someone pushes through the turnstile. With a clear and correct state model, you can implement a centralized object to manage state transitions and then use it exclusively.

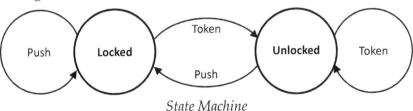

State Machine

Model state and implement a centralized object to manage state transitions.

Not Reflecting State Change Right Away

After starting an import, the progress indicator does not change.

After a new task is assigned, it does not appear in the task list until the page has been refreshed.

While viewing the active order list, changes by other users do not cause the status to update.

Web pages that keep status up to date are nice, but this behavior only comes because you engineered them that way. When state changes are not reflected (or not reflected soon enough), this is evidence of missing or inadequate status reporting between server and web client. Consider where state changes take place on the back end and how they are communicated to the front end. One technique is to refresh a page after performing a server action to show the new state. For longer-running processes, a page can make regular asynchronous calls to the server to check whether there is any change in state to show. You'll want to make these checks often enough to show status changes reasonably quickly, but not so often that the server is overloaded with requests.

Confused Form State

When an order submit fails due to an error, the Submit button is not re-enabled and it is impossible to re-submit the order.

After selecting a non-US country, country is reset back to US when user clicks on Save button and there are validation errors on other fields.

One common problem with web form state is the failed submit: when a submit is rejected due to an error, failure to reset the state of the form can result in problems with form elements such as lack of visibility or incorrect enabled/disabled state. It's easy to see how these problems arise, because developers often disable much of a form while a submit is being processed so users don't interact with the form. Other times the form is re-initialized after an error to defaults, which loses the user's input.

A failed submit should display an error message but otherwise return the form to the condition it was in before the submit button was clicked. It's helpful to centralize visual element state changes in a handful of JavaScript functions that can easily be called to initialize/reset a form, disable some elements when a submit starts, or report an error.

Inability to Restore to a Known State

The Restore Default Preferences button is not restoring all settings.

After accidentally dragging the wrong item to the shopping cart, there is no way to remove it.

Clicking on Undo button fails to revert last item added/updated.

How much control you give users over state depends on what your application does, but it's generally a good idea to be forgiving about accidental user interactions and provide a way to revert them. Any user might select the wrong item or click the wrong element at times; and some users have accessibility challenges.

Applications with many options should consider a way to reset back to default settings, or support the concept of templates. With templates, users can save combinations of options and you can provide pre-built templates for common scenarios.

Over-caching

After uploading a new user avatar image, the previous image is still displayed everywhere in the application.

The order status page does not show the true status unless the browse cache is cleared and the page is refreshed.

Good use of caching is a major factor in boosting web application performance, but over-caching can get in the way of showing the latest state or content. This problem is multiplied further with the use of Content Delivery Networks (CDNs), where an item such as an image might be cached for a week.

The best things to cache are items that won't change or won't change often, such as application images, CSS files, and JavaScript files. Web pages with dynamic content should not be cached. For anything you cache that might need to be updated, you need a way to force a cache update. You can do that by changing the URL, or by carefully setting the cache expiration date.

Invalid Saved Page State

When returning to the dashboard, some tiles are placed in incorrect locations and can't be modified.

When returning to the task list after upgrading to v3 of the software, the displayed tasks have missing due dates.

Pages and forms that persist state are useful: when a user returns to the page, they are back to where they left off. However, if improper state has somehow been saved then the user may be caught in an ugly situation when revisiting a page that contains unexpected values.

Invalid state can result from bugs in saving persistence; from modifying the stored data; or from older state data that doesn't match the newer software. Use a versioning scheme to handle changes to persisted state data. When restoring saved state for a page, never trust that it is correct: instead, practice defensive programming and validate the persisted data, discarding any incorrect values.

Idempotency Problems

In software, *idempotence* refers to operations that have no side effects if called more than once with the same parameters. For example, imagine you have software with a submit order operation. On some systems, if you submit an order and later call submit order a second time with the exact same parameters that will result in another new order. In contrast, an idempotent implementation will only create one order no matter how many times the call is made.

Idempotence is a particularly valuable characteristic in web applications because your server-side application cannot control what web requests a client (or hacker or tester) might make. With an idempotent implementation, your software is considerably more resilient to abuse.

The concept of idempotence combines well with RESTful services but requires intentional design. One common approach is to use unique identifiers so repeated requests which have already been processed can be detected and ignored.

Design services to be idempotent.

Idempotency Failure

Repeating a web request to generate and mail a monthly statement results in the creation of additional emails each time it is called.

Use unique identifiers in requests, and track requests in the database. When a request is processed, ignore duplicate requests that have already been performed.

Failure to Enforce Uniqueness

User can create more than one document with the same name in the same folder.

Check whether an existing name/ID is in use before allowing a new one to be created. Use an underlying storage mechanism such as a database primary key for name/ID, which will disallow duplicates.

Security Problems

Security problems can be intrinsic, where they reveal a foundational problem such as an insecure design. The more secure the design, the more central your security mechanisms are.

Security problems can also be due to an omission, such as a developer forgetting to follow the security policy at times. For example, if every web server action is supposed to validate the correctness of URL query parameters, but one action fails to do so, then a vulnerability has been created. Whenever possible, centralize your security mechanisms so that you are not depending on developers remembering to do something throughout the code: opt-out security is superior to opt-in security.

When a good security foundation is in place, security problems usually indicate vulnerability to a specific type of attack. The answer is to understand the attack well, and add a defense that mitigates it.

Make your security as centralized as possible. Avoid opt-in security mechanisms.

Spoofing Identity Attacks

A hacker was easily able to guess sign-in usernames.

A hacker was able to learn passwords with a dictionary attack.

A tester was able to access the Production system because she knew the developers commonly use the password "12345" for test accounts.

A hacker was able to access the root account of our web server because the admin username and password had never been changed from the defaults.

Multiple user sessions on the same machine are confusing user identity. Logging in as a second user showed the identity from the first user session.

Do not give away information in error messages that tells a hacker which input field was correct or incorrect. Don't display credentials or leave them in a web page.

A weak password is pretty much the same as no password to an experienced hacker. Use strong passwords that cannot be easily guessed. Never use hard-coded passwords, default passwords, or widely-known passwords. It's common in developer and test environments to use simple developer/test passwords that "everyone knows"—but it is fatal to allow any of that to make its way into Production. Similarly, be sure to change the default password on all servers, databases, and other accounts. Also consider what your password expiration policy should be; how many login attempts you will allow before locking an account; and whether to include two-factor authentication.

Strongly encrypt session cookies so they cannot be easily reverse-engineered.

Be sure your security session model holds up to real-world conditions, such as multiple web browser sessions on the same machine.

Tampering with Data Attacks

A user was able to edit an order they should not have been able to by changing the order number in a URL.

A user was able to apply a discount offer that should not have been available to them, by using F12 web developer tools and JavaScript to change the values in a select list.

A user was able to change data by re-playing a web session captured from another user.

For web applications, your server actions should never assume that web requests and body payloads are validated, even if your own web pages normally perform validation. A malicious user can tamper with pages and web requests. Server actions should always perform independent validation of input and authorization checks. Never trust that a value will be correct because your web page only offered valid choices; the form data may have been altered.

To thwart replay attacks, always use SSL. Disallow non-SSL web traffic or redirect it to SSL.

SQL Injection Attacks

A user was able to delete orders by adding SQL script to the end of an input field.

A user was able to list customer information by adding SQL script to the end of an input field.

Dynamic SQL involves assembling database queries from form input. This practice is very dangerous: if a clever user adds additional SQL statements to the input, you could be executing malicious code such as a command to delete records or drop tables. It is far preferable to use mechanisms known to be secure, such as SQL parameters and stored procedures.

If you must perform dynamic SQL, take measures to protect against SQL injection. If input contains a semicolon (starting a new SQL statement), disallow everything past it. Screen for dangerous commands such as DROP and DELETE and TRUNCATE and reject the input.

Repudiation Attack

A user was able to delete all orders and later deny it; there was no evidence logged to show whether they did it or not.

A user was able to get the log of their activities to record a different username.

To audit activity, it must be logged. Logging of activity should be done server-side in a way that client actions cannot subvert the accuracy of the logging. Auditing should reliably track user identity, timestamp, and action performed; and any additional information that might be useful such as the user's IP address.

Information Disclosure Attack

A user was able to learn the names of database tables by deliberately inducing an add record error with invalid form data.

A user was able to get to records of other employees by specifying their employee Id numbers in a search.

A hacker was able to access our database.

Defenses against information disclosure need to consider several categories of protected information. Avoid giving away anything about application internals to a user, such as database names or a stack trace. Instead log appropriate error detail but display friendly error messages devoid of information useful to a hacker.

Users should only be allowed to see information they are authorized for, even if they are clever enough to change URLs or tinker with web requests. Server-side actions should always perform authorization checks. Even when a user is authorized to see records, consider that they may not be authorized to see all of it. It's particularly important to protect personally-identifiable information (PII) and other sensitive information.

Information disclosure can also result from poorly-defended infrastructure such as servers and databases. Use solid credentials that use strong passwords and steer clear of widely-known or default passwords; and keep the credentials secret. Avoid storing passwords, database connection strings, and other sensitive information in plain text; and never display them. Use firewalls to disallow external access to servers and databases, whether in the enterprise or in the cloud.

Denial of Service Attack

A user was able to crash the application server.

A user was able to slow down the app significantly by sending many repeated requests.

Denial of service is tough to defend against. Learn what defenses are offered by your hosting infrastructure, then add your own additional defenses.

If your application server crashes, the best defense is redundancy: a farm of servers will keep your application available. In cloud environments, health monitoring and recycling may be built in to VMs.

In a cloud web farm scenario, if you are being flooded with requests consider having dynamic scale in place so that you can still service users in the short term while you deal with stopping the attack. Of course, you need to put an upper limit on how large you scale in order to keep costs within reason.

None of the above will fully defend against denial of service attacks. Monitoring of availability and health is essential so that you can recognize attacks early and notify a support engineer to take action.

Session Fixation Attack

A user was able to re-use a session by observing web traffic and emulating it.

A user was able to re-use a session by capturing and re-playing web traffic.

When your web sessions are created, however you identify them, take steps to ensure they are idempotent and cannot be re-used. For example, if you track sessions in a database with unique Ids and create session cookies based on those records, consider having an "IsRedeemed" field that gets set once a session is used; your code can then refuse to register an already-redeemed session a second time.

Elevation of Privilege Attack

A user who was not signed in was able to directly browse to pages meant only for employees.

A user was able to browse to administrator pages even though they were not an administrator.

Ensure individual web server actions are properly secured, and don't make the assumption that a user will not have learned your URL organization. A user who is not signed in should be limited to just a few areas, such as a login page. Areas that require a specific role need to be locked down.

In legacy apps that have been upgraded, check that older areas of the software do not allow newer security mechanisms to be bypassed.

Performance Problems

It takes multiple minutes for a user to sign-in.

The Inventory Report is really slow, especially when run in the evenings.

Searches often take 30+ seconds to complete.

Performance problems can be a real headache to developers, especially when not planned for and tested during the development phase.

Performance problems that are readily reproducible are easiest to study, whereas wildly varying performance requires deep analysis to understand the factors and dynamics involved. Since performance is highly subjective, developers benefit most from precise information, such as specific performance targets in requirements. Likewise, specific information in bug reports is most helpful, such as specific actions taken and wait times experienced. Vague descriptions such as "the system is slow" are of little use.

Insufficient Hardware

If your software and its usage exceeds the capacity of hardware it is running on, performance will suffer. A more robust server with faster processor, more cores, more memory, or faster disk drives may be in order. If running on a VM, consider increasing the memory of the VM. Measure CPU and I/O to determine where the real problem is.

If your servers run in a farm and you have too few servers for the number of users, performance will be poor. In cloud environments, you can usually set up auto-scaling, such that the number of VMs is increased or decreased based on load. Auto-scaling works best when you can establish hard limits on the minimum and maximum number of servers: this keeps costs in line, and ensures that a minimum farm size has a reasonable amount of redundancy.

Network Latency

Many applications today are distributed, which means the network plays a critical role in performance. Check that your network is up to the task: if it has poor capacity or is overloaded, an upgrade is in order. In the same way, poor Internet connectivity can impede performance. You may not be able to control every part of an Internet connection, but the parts of the infrastructure you can control need to have adequate capacity.

Environmental Changes

A change in environment can impact performance noticeably. A change in hardware could help performance but could also hurt it. An upgrade to an operating system or server software can similarly sometimes help and sometimes hurt. Adding or changing anti-virus software can affect performance.

Performance problems that are most severe during certain times of day, days of the week, or days of the month may indicate that other processes are also running that impact performance. For example, a database backup might be taking place during evening hours.

If you are running in a VM and you share your server with

other VMs, the activities of other tenants could affect you.

Default Configurations

Many server products are shipped with default configurations that are not optimal for live production. For example, some web server software arrives in a default configuration with many features disabled or set to low thresholds, in the name of security. If your server products are not configured well for production, your performance and server capacity can be impacted. Follow production-readiness guidelines for your server to tune the configuration.

Dependencies on Other Systems

A performance problem may come from a dependency on another system. For example, an airline reservation service might have high latency at times.

One strategy for this kind of issue is to perform the communication in the background so the user does not have to wait. This isn't always appropriate, however, such as when you need to wait for completion of the communication before the user can proceed.

Changes in User Patterns

Some perceived performance problems are simply the result of a change in user patterns. For example, the start of a benefits enrollment period might see a large increase in user activity. See the section on Increased Load for ideas on how to respond to changes in load.

Increased Load

In order to respond to changes in load you need to be measuring load. Some different measurements you can use as a basis for knowing when to increase capacity are CPU utilization, average response time, queue length, average time to complete a transaction, and transactions per time-period. For example, you might set up a rule that when average CPU utilization exceeds 60% on your server farm, it's time to add another server. You could similarly have a complementary rule that when server utilization drops below 20%, it's time to remove a server.

If you are hosting a farm of servers in a cloud environment, you can use auto-scaling to add more servers when load increases and drop servers when load decreases. You'll want to do this with a fixed upper and lower limit to the number of servers, in order to control costs on the high end and have sufficient availability on the low end.

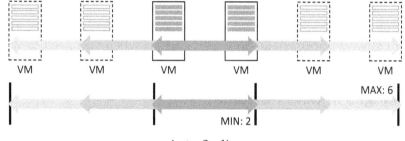

Auto-Scaling

Redundant Activity

Inefficient or improper code can perform activities more often than necessary. For example, a poor understanding of web page events can lead to event handlers firing more often than the developer anticipated; this in turn might lead to extraneous Ajax calls to server actions, noticeably affecting response times.

Inefficient Algorithms

Inefficient algorithms can compromise performance. Replace them with an efficient algorithm. For example, a bubble sort is simple to code but highly inefficient sorting algorithm; replacing it with a more efficient algorithm such as Quick Sort will improve performance.

Code that performs unnecessary work should also be avoided.

Overly-complex Code

Overly-complex code is likely to be inefficient code. Determining where the offending areas of code are can be challenging; temporarily adding logging code can be helpful in finding bottlenecks. Refactoring is recommended both to discover the problem areas and to improve them.

Inefficient Web Pages

Web pages can be real performance hogs simply by not being efficient. Bundling and minifying CSS and JavaScript files will dramatically reduce page size and reduce the number of HTTP requests. Caching often-used files such as image files will also reduce the number of HTTP requests made over time.

Failure to Leverage Caching

Caching is one of the easiest ways to noticeably boost performance with minimal effort. However, it needs to be done carefully: caching the wrong things, or caching without any way to update content can be as bad as failing to cache.

For web applications, you typically do not want to cache HTML pages (since they can change) but do want to cache images, CSS files, and JavaScript files (since they rarely change). You can cache with far-future expiration dates to keep content cached for long periods of time; however, you should also have a way to force a cache update when cached content does change. You can force a cache update by changing a content file's URL slightly, such as adding a version number. You can usually reference a CDN for popular third-party CSS and JS files like jQuery and

Bootstrap, which serves up content efficiently no matter where a user is located. You can get the same benefit for your own content by hosting it in a CDN.

Inefficient Database Design and Queries

Missing indexes or improper indexes are a common cause of application performance problems. Even carefully designed databases can run afoul of this when additional fields are added later on and there is a failure to consider indexing. Database profiling tools can help uncover opportunities for query optimization.

Another frequent problem is querying for too much data. A SELECT * query against a large record is wasteful if just a few columns are actually going to be used from the results. Database queries should only retrieve the information they need.

Inefficient Formats

Like programming languages, data formats is an area where there are many opinions. For example, let's take XML: some have a high opinion of it while others view it with distaste. It's certainly valid to factor in experience and available tools when making format decisions, but there's more than preference involved here: regardless of its other merits, markup formats such as XML are undeniably large and sometimes costly to process. That means if you use XML, you should realize it's going to have a performance impact.

Developers sometimes have no choice in the data formats they have to work with, but when you do have a choice efficiency should be a primary consideration. Consider the alternatives before committing to a format.

Unnecessary Data Conversion

As data flows between the tiers of your application, it may change form. Sometimes this is necessary, but when it isn't that can cause performance problems. Consider an application whose server retrieves large amounts of information from an XML web service, then passes that same information to a web client as JSON. That may be a situation you can do nothing about, but when you are in a position to change it consider the gains you can get from avoiding unnecessary conversions.

Unbounded Growth

Resources that grow without limits eventually cause problems which can manifest as performance problems or outright failures. That includes unbounded memory growth as well as unbounded data growth.

To keep memory growth in check, avoid both memory leaks and dynamic arrays without bounding rules. While memory leaks are less of a concern when using modern languages with garbage collection, they are still possible when references are not released, or when APIs provide handles that are not released. Dynamic arrays and collections should not be permitted unmanaged growth: items need to have their lifetime managed and be removed when no longer needed.

To keep data in check, consider what the lifetime should be for older data. Archive and delete older data once it is no longer needed. Failure to do this can increase query time and increase the time required for maintenance activities such as backup and restoration.

Serial Activities that Can be Parallelized

A series of processing steps that are taking longer than desired may be a candidate for parallelization, if the steps are not dependent on order of completion. For example, consider a function that posts a comment to 3 different social networks on behalf of a user. Each operation takes some time due to Internet communication. As there are no dependencies between the operations, they can safely be performed in parallel in a thread pool.

Inefficient Use of Transactions and Synchronization

Transactions and other forms of synchronization guard resources against parallel updates. If these mechanisms are used too broadly or carelessly, performance can be affected by the unnecessary waiting; or deadlock can ensue.

Failure to Pool Resources

It is inefficient to frequently re-create resources when they could be pooled. For example, consider a function that calls several other functions, each of which open a connection to the same database, perform some work, and close the connection. Pooling the connection would be more efficient than creating and releasing multiple connections.

Queue Servicing

When information is queued to be performed but the work is not being processed sufficiently quickly, the queue length will grow, likely resulting in a visible performance problem to those waiting on completion of their work items.

Queue service time can be improved by increasing the number of workers servicing the queue or by making the queue servicing code more efficient.

If important work is being delayed when lesser tasks are in the queue, consider assigning a priority to queue items. If your queuing system doesn't have a feature for priority of task, you can use a separate queue for high- and low-priority items. Workers can service the low priority queue only when there are no tasks to process in the high-priority queue.

Excessive Logging

Logging is extremely useful for capturing error detail, aiding problem analysis, and auditing activity. It can also hurt performance when done excessively. In general, poor places for logging are sections of code that are frequently called, and within loops.

Intermittent Problems

Intermittent problems are those that only occur "sometimes". This can mean that the conditions for failure have not been fully identified by the testers. The first response should be additional analysis, which will often tell you more. With your knowledge of the internal implementation, you may sometimes see patterns in the failures that would not be evident to the tester.

When analysis has failed to identify clear conditions for failure, you may be faced with a *race condition*. In a race condition, events do not happen in the order anticipated by the developer. Race conditions are often difficult to diagnose because observing them can change their behavior. For this reason, these kinds of bugs are sometimes called "Heisenbugs" in reference to the Heisenberg Observer Effect. You may not be able to reproduce race conditions with a debugger as that will affect the timing. Simpler mechanisms such as logging are often helpful in finding where the problem lies. If you're not making headway, get some additional developers involved and put your heads together.

Race conditions can occur when the developer has made assumptions about timing and order of activities that are not always predictable, or that are very different in the target environment from the development environment. Code should not assume how long it will take a thread or network operation or database update to complete. Instead, use signal mechanisms such as events to confirm an activity has completed, and structure code so that there is no question processing is happening in the proper order. Shared state between multiple threads can also be can also be a cause of race conditions. Use synchronization mechanisms such as semaphores or mutexes to control how critical sections of code update shared state.

Avoid race conditions by not making assumptions about timing or the order of activities. Use events to signal completion of activities. Use synchronization mechanisms to update shared state.

In JavaScript code, race conditions can happen when you perform non-immediate actions such as Ajax requests within a loop, where values of variables may be different by the time your Ajax success function executes. You can guard against that kind of problem by calling a function to perform the Ajax operation and passing in variables as parameters.

Similar to race conditions are parallel activity problems, where one activity interferes with another. For example, a shopping cart checkout process might work perfectly when tested for a single user but fail when two users are trying to buy the same item in parallel and inventory levels are low. Unless you're okay with some degree of "overbooking", you can resolve this kind of conflict by locking a resource in some way so it cannot be doubly reserved. If that's not feasible, then you should check resource availability not only at the start of a process but at every step of the process. Even if you deliberately allow overbooking, it will be necessary to build in a resolution mechanism such as making refunds.

Race Conditions

Bulk operations on a group of selected orders sometimes work and sometimes do not.

After uploading a document, an immediate attempt to view the document sometimes fails.

In a race condition, code can succeed or fail due a dependency on timing. This happens because several streams of code need to be synchronized so that they cooperate with each other.

One type of race condition is a lack of synchronization between parallel threads. For example, if two threads are both updating and using the same variable without synchronization, unexpected behavior can result. If the threads use a synchronization mechanism such as a critical section, they can coordinate access without conflicts.

Another type of race condition is caused by calling functions the developer does not realize are asynchronous. For example, calling a library function to upload a document to a document repository then immediately calling another library function to retrieve the document contents, where the library functions are asynchronous but the developer is unaware; this could succeed or fail based on timing. The code must wait for the asynchronous function to complete before additional logic executes. Use an asynchronous pattern appropriate for the language you are using.

When developers first realize they have a race condition they sometime compensate by adding a delay, such as sleeping for a few seconds. This is not a proper correction: a different environment or different load could change the amount of delay needed. The right thing to do is coordinate processing through a synchronization mechanism such as semaphores, mutexes, or critical sections; or by the use of events to signal completion of processing.

When synchronization is needed at the database level, transactions are the standard solution. A transaction takes a batch of database operations and treats them as a single unit of work. Transactions have the properties of being atomic, consistent, isolated, and durable (ACID).

Usability Problems

Page is Too Large / Too Noisy

Overly-busy pages impede usability: there's too much to focus on, increasing the likelihood something will be missed; and users have a hard time finding their way around.

If possible, remove "noise" from the page:
- Remove or reduce content. Eliminate verbosity. Re-work long sentences and paragraphs to be shorter and clearer.
- Avoid repetitive content.
- Remove or soften overly-prominent images.
- Soften blatant typography and reduce the number of different fonts in use.
- Reduce the number of colors, or find a more agreeable combination of colors.
- Space content that is too close-together farther apart.
- Arrange the more important content to be more prominent on the page.

If you're having difficulty de-cluttering a busy page even after applying the above tips, it may be necessary to break the page into several pages.

Users Have Difficulty Finding Things

Users can't find how to edit their profile or change their profile picture.

I couldn't find the New Properties Report, because the menu item for it was not grouped with the other reports.

If users are having a hard time finding an area of the software, that either means navigation to it is confusing, is hidden, or the area does not exist. Ensure there is straightforward navigation to every area.

If you have multi-level navigation, avoid too many levels and group menu sub-items logically: *Sign Out* doesn't belong under *Products*. Use clear wording: on a criminology site, does *Profile* refer to criminal profiles or the user's profile? Functions available under icons or toolbar buttons should either be accompanied by text or have tooltip help.

Even with well-designed navigation some users will have trouble at times. Provide a site search facility so a user who is struggling with navigation has another way to find what they need.

Even when a user finds what they need in the application, they may be hesitant to click it if they are uncertain about what will happen next. When the consequence of clicking something is unclear, that leads to *click fear*, which discourages users from exploring the application. Click fear can paralyze your user base. When you communicate options and actions to a user, be sure to set clear expectations.

Unclear or Inconsistent Terminology

American users have not been using the CV Upload facility because they are more used to the term "resume".

Candidates have not been applying for job openings because we call them "requisitions" on the job site.

Use clear terminology. Terms presented to users should be the terms that are most familiar to your target users, not the programmers. The best terms are not always the same for all personas. HR Recruiters might relate to the term Requisitions but a candidate on a job site will more readily respond to Job Opening.

In the same way, users who speak the same language but are in different locales can need different terms: English is spoken in the US and in the UK, but what is known as a *wrench* in the US is a *spanner* in the UK. In language support, be sure to associate users with locales (language + location), not just language

Users can also be confused when you waffle between multiple terms for the same thing. Use terms consistently: don't call a home a *house* in some places and a *residence* in others.

User-unfriendly Error Messages

Error code 0x8107005

Your credit card was declined.

Validation error: improper date format

Null reference exception

System.InvalidOperationException: Error during serialization or deserialization using the JSON JavaScriptSerializer. The length of the string exceeds the value set on the maxJsonLength property.

System.Xml.XmlException: Data at the root level is invalid. Line 1, position 1. at System.Xml.XmlTextReaderImpl.Throw(String res, String arg) at System.Xml.XmlTextReaderImpl.ParseRootLevelWhitespace() at System.Xml.XmlTextReaderImpl.ParseDocumentContent() at System.Xml.XmlReader.MoveToContent() at System.Data.DataSet.ReadXml(XmlReader reader, Boolean denyResolving) at CommerceBoost.ParseApplication.ReadXml(Stream stream)

Error messages should always be user-friendly. Error messages that include technical details (such as an error code or a stack trace) are a double-fail: they are unhelpful to the user and could also reveal internal details to a hacker. Technical detail about errors should be logged, not displayed.

Error messages should be spelled correctly and use proper grammar, not sentence fragments. A good error message is clearly worded and avoids giving the user the wrong idea. If a user just attempted to submit a form and the error message is *Submit failed*, how does the user know where they stand? Should they resubmit?

The most helpful error messages also provide the user some information about cause or recourse. The wording of a message like *Your credit card was declined* may cause a user to think there is a problem with their card when the issue may just be a typo on a payment form. If there's space for it, a better message would be *Your credit card information was declined by the processor. Please check the correctness of your billing address and credit card number, and that sufficient funds are available.*

Even messages that are thought to be user-friendly may fail to be effective if the choice of wording is poor. If a form submit fails because a user entered an invalid date, a message like *Validation Error: Improper Date Format* is overkill when *Please enter a valid date* would suffice.

EPILOGUE

Evan was a young developer new to the project team. He had been told he needed to spend time with a lead developer who had an amazing reputation for quality. Evan couldn't think of a subject more boring, and certainly didn't feel he needed a mentor—but he was curious: if half the stories he heard were to be believed, this man could walk on water.

He entered the man's office, a few minutes early, and sat down. There was a biography of Antonius Stradivarius on the desk, and a sign that said "The Bug Stops Here." If the calendar on the wall was any indication, this man actually had free time for leisure activities. Despite himself, Evan started to become interested.

A minute later, a friendly man entered and shook Evan's hand warmly. "Hello," said the man. "My name is Jon."

GLOSSARY

accessibility testing testing alternative methods of interacting with the software, usually to facilitate users with disabilities.

assertion a declaration of a condition that should be true.

automated testing testing driven by an automation tool, requiring no interaction by a human being.

automated UI test an automated test of the user interface that simulates human interaction.

automated API test an automated test that invokes an API or service.

backlog item a feature to be developed in the software.

baseline an initial set of test results, used in benchmarking.

benchmark a set of test results, compared against a baseline.

black box testing testing based on requirements or ad-hoc usage, without any knowledge of the internal implementation.

bohrbug a consistent, repeatable bug.

broken window an aspect of the software that is broken, sloppy, or incomplete that should be taken care of in order to keep the neighborhood respectable.

bug a defect or perceived defect in the software.

bug category a defect classification, useful in analyzing problem areas for a developer or a team.

bug churn back-and-forth handing off of a bug between QA and developer.

bug qualification confirming a bug is valid before acting on it.

build system a system for automated compilation of the software, that can build software on-demand or on a schedule.

bundling a technique to combine multiple CSS or JavaScript files into a single file in order to reduce the number of web requests.

code debt code that needs to be written.

cohesion the degree to which the elements of a module belong together.

compatibility testing testing that determines software fitness in a particular hardware/software environment.

compliance testing an audit to determine whether the software meets a defined standard.

condition of acceptance a condition that must be satisfied in order for a story to be accepted as complete and correct.

conditions of failure the conditions under which a bug occurs.

continuous integration (CI) use of test automation in the build system to validate source control check-ins and reject breaking changes.

continuous improvement dedication to continual self-improvement.

continuous quality being mindful of quality at all times.

corner case a condition where more than one edge case is in effect at the same time.

coupling how dependent software components are on each other.

craftsman a highly-skilled artisan who upholds a certain level of workmanship.

decision table a table used to model rules, conditions and actions.

defensive programming techniques that ensure software continues to function despite unforeseen circumstances.

definition of done a checklist of activities that all need to be completed in order to really be considered done.

denial of service making the application unavailable to valid users.

dependency injection (DI) a design pattern for isolating dependencies, typically by passing an object its instance variables.

developer testing testing performed by software developers prior to turning the software over to QA for formal test.

don't repeat yourself (DRY) a principle for eliminating redundancy which states that every piece of knowledge must have a single, unambiguous, authoritative representation within a system.

edge case a value at or beyond the extreme minimum or maximum of allowable values.

elevation of privilege a user gaining an unauthorized level of access.

epic a master story, decomposed into a series of detail stories.

equivalent functionality attack following more than one path to the same activity to see if there are any differences in behavior.

expected behavior in a bug report, what the test expected to happen.

fault injection forcing errors into code dynamically at compile time or runtime.

functional testing positive use case testing to confirm requirements have been satisfied and conditions of acceptance have been met.

fuzz testing use of automation to generate random data.

heisenbug a bug that defies analysis.

hindenbug a bug with catastrophic consequences.

hostile testing testing that attempts to cause failures through incorrect or unexpected use.

implementation the code written by a developer to implement a story.

information disclosure: making information available to users who are not authorized to have it.

integration testing testing combinations of units of software.

iterate to repeat and refine.

load testing testing that a system can operate under a specific level of load.

localization adapting software to serve the needs of a specific language, locale, or culture.

mandelbug a bug with chaotic behavior and complex causes.

manual testing testing through human interaction and observation.

minification code optimization for CSS and JavaScript that removes unnecessary white space and comments and shortens variable names.

monkey testing use of automation to generate random interactions and data.

observed behavior in a bug report, what the tester observed that was different from the *expected behavior*.

optimization removal of inefficiencies and imperfections.

performance testing testing that measures availability, responsiveness, processing speed, scalability, or stability of the solution.

profiling tool a dynamic code analysis tool that identifies performance bottlenecks.

quality bar a minimum standard for acceptable quality.

quality gate a person or mechanism that enforces a quality bar.

refactor restructuring code to have an improved organization without affecting its external behavior.

repro steps a list of steps that can be followed to reproduce a bug.

repudiation denial that a malicious action was performed or attempted.

requirement a thing that is needed or wanted.

root cause analysis the underlying cause behind a defect.

security testing testing that focuses on authentication, authorization, auditing, and data privacy considerations.

separation of concerns (SoC) a principle for separating functionality into distinct areas with as little overlap as possible.

schrödinbug a problem you didn't know you had with running software.

single responsibility principle (SRP) a principle that states a class or module should have one and only one responsibility, and be the only thing with that responsibility.

source control a repository for safe-keeping of program code that maintains a history of changes.

sprint a project work cycle.

spoofing identity accessing and using another user's authentication information.

SQL injection attack entering SQL script into an input field in the hopes it will be executed.

story a description of a requirement.

stress testing testing reliability under heavy workloads.

suggestion bug a logged bug that contains a suggestion from the tester, not a defect in the software.

system testing testing the complete system.

tampering with data malicious modification of data.

test verifying whether something that should be so is actually so.

test automation pyramid a hierarchy of software levels to be tested through automation.

test coverage the percentage of the software for which tests exist.

test-first development creating a test for a unit of software before it is implemented.

test plan a test script that includes initialization to a known state, a sequence of steps to perform, and conditions to check.

unit testing testing small atomic units of software.

usability testing testing user responses to the solution to gauge usability.

user acceptance testing (UAT) testing of the near-final solution with some of the intended users of the system.

user interface testing testing the user-facing parts of the software.

white box testing testing informed by a knowledge of the internal implementation.

INDEX

INDEX

ABOUT THE AUTHOR

David Pallmann has been developing software professionally for over 35 years, and has worked on a wide range of software solutions including desktop publishing systems, enterprise server products, developer tools, APIs, web sites, mobile apps, and cloud-based SaaS solutions. He has served in many project roles including product owner, development manager, architect, developer, visual designer, and tester.

He resides in Southern California with his wife Becky, their three children, and assorted pets (currently a German Shepherd, a Bearded Dragon, and fish).

www.ingramcontent.com/pod-product-compliance
Lightning Source LLC
Chambersburg PA
CBHW071545080326
40689CB00061B/1846